The Concept of Sin

The Concept of Sin

Josef Pieper

Translated by Edward T. Oakes, S.J.

St. Augustine's Press
South Bend, Indiana
2001

Library of Congress Cataloging in Publication Data
Pieper, Josef, 1904–
    [Über den Begriff der Sünde. English]
    The concept of sin / by Josef Pieper ; translated by
    Edward T. Oakes.
       p. cm.
    Includes bibliographical references and index.
    ISBN 1-890318-07-8 (alk. paper) – ISBN 1-890318-08-6
    (pbk. : alk. paper)
    1. Sin. 2. Catholic Church – Doctrines. I. Title.
BT715 .P5313 2000
241'.4 – dc21   00-010787

Table of Contents

Contents

VIII
The Stain of Sin

What remains after the sinful act is over – *Macula*, guilt, liability
to punishment – Atonement as a chance to purge guilt – The
problematic reliance on punishment decreed by man – The
"eternity-intention" in deadly sin – "Hell" as self-imprisonment
with the prisoner holding the key – The prerequisite for forgiveness: recognizing and repenting one's own guilt – Contrition;
self-accusation; confession – Man's autonomous self-under-
standing and the attitude of the "fallen angels" – The necessity
for a divine act of forgiveness.

Translator's Preface

As a professional translator, I had always assumed I preferred literal over periphrastic renderings – until, that is, I took on the assignment of translating Josef Pieper. Although his tone of voice is quite pastoral and warm, even avuncular, he exploits a feature of German academic style to the full that could never be literally transferred to English: the use of participles – both active and passive and drawn from both transitive and intransitive verbs – as substantives. The American philosopher John Dewey once asked aloud if the German fondness for nouns over verbs as shown in the German proclivity for turning participles into substantives and capitalizing all nouns might indicate something suspicious about Teutonic metaphysics.

Be that as it may, Josef Pieper's own proclivities in that regard have to be broken down into something more flowing if the English-speaking reader is not to feel that he has sat down at the bibliographical equivalent of a German meal, having to digest more potato dumplings than his own leaner diet requires.

German also favors, as a kind of *digestif*, a large number of connectives ("furthermore," "indeed," "on the contrary," etc.) and sentence adverbs ("certainly," "perhaps," etc.) and concessives ("nonetheless," "and yet," etc.). English idiom tends to leave such logical signals implied in the argument, perhaps because the sentences are not so lumpy and "dumpling-esque" to begin with.

I mention all of this to thank two friends who read over the manuscript in draft. The first, my colleague John Kane, had the yeoman's work to do, because for the first draft I had followed my usual practice of working up a literal translation, and it fell to him to provide the needed "first encounter." He is also an avid reader of Pieper's works in English, and so could also provide good advice as to the tone of voice I needed to capture.

After following (most of) his advice, I then gave the manuscript to my Jesuit *confrère* Fr. Edward L. Maginnis, who continued to spot further infelicities and errors. In both cases, I told them that I would have to check their recommendations against the original German, so they should not be held for any other clumsiness that might yet cling to the translation, although I am perfectly happy to attribute any fluent grace the text might have to their generous assistance.

Let me also add that, as a salve to my literalist conscience, I tried as much as possible to translate only sentence by sentence. Only in the case of the first paragraph of the book did I feel I had to take even more liberties in order to break down any initial feeling of Teutonic cadence that the translation still had. Catching the reader's attention and enthusiasm seemed more important than plodding along like a Hegel wannabe.

But at all times I knew that my main responsibility as a translator was to convey the *precision* of the author's thought. As a true disciple of St. Thomas, Pieper knows when to draw the relevant distinction and when to concede that further analysis would only repeat the hairsplitting that remains the popular impression of *all* medieval philosophy *tout court*. But weariness with oversubtle distinctions must never justify sloppy or indistinct thinking. As St. Ignatius Loyola says in a letter (11 September 1536) to Teresa Rejadell, "a person with imprecise ideas can understand little and be of less help to others." Josef Pieper understands much, and so his book, I am sure, will be of great benefit to all readers.

For that reason – that is, because I wanted to make his fascinating book as useful as possible to that mythical beast, the "general reader" – I also took the liberty of providing more elaborate identifications of people and technical terms (especially Latin terms) than are present in the original. For example, the author mentions somewhat in passing the name Jürgen Moltmann, whom I then further identify by describing him as an important Protestant theologian after World War II. To avoid unnecessary distractions or overloading the book with too many endnotes, I placed such epexigetical phrases (and sometimes sentences) in the text "silently," since I felt certain none of these "additions" affect the original meaning at all. I have also provided titles to each of the chapters. Pieper usually makes his Tables of Contents serve as a kind of running index or initial reconnoitering of the terrain; but chapter titles seemed to me helpful to my mythical menagerie, so I went ahead and supplied them.

The Pedantry Police might object to these strategies, but I have recently renewed my official Translator's License, which, like the Poet's License, gives a citizen in the Republic of Letters all kinds of immunity from arrest – although the reader should know that at one point I have

tried the patience of the Court: the quote from John
Milton's *Paradise Lost* in the last chapter comes from me
and not the author: *pecca fortiter.*

Edward T. Oakes, S.J.
Regis University
Denver, Colorado
14 September 2000
Feast of the Triumph of the Cross

I
Usage

We don't hear the word "sin" much anymore. Or so it would seem. At first glance, this observation can be easily verified: an average, ordinary conversation overheard at random will hardly ever mention the term. Of course no one expects to hear a somber word like "sin" when people are just rattling on in their casual, everyday "chit-chat." But even when they are engaged in serious discussions about pressing issues of the day, talking earnestly in such "high-toned" settings as salons, classrooms, or broadcasting studios – where the concept would seem more appropriate – no, even here the word "sin" can find no place.

Why is it that we seem to find it difficult, if not downright impossible, to speak in impartial, matter-of-fact tones of sin? Upon reflection, it would seem rather odd to speak of sin using inflections no different from those we use when we are talking about the tangible things of everyday life. But odder yet is that, even when we are giving verbal expression to the specific content of our inner life – when the conversation turns to such topics as conscience, or justice, or death – the word "sin" rarely crops up. Obviously there is something about the topic that keeps us from invoking the word "sin" without exposing ourselves to the raised eyebrow or perhaps even to rhetorical "assault."

Could this remarkable irritation in the word have

something to do with the reality that this deceptively simple morpheme means and names? In a speech delivered shortly after the First World War (one that has since become rather notorious and which he gave, no doubt with a certain irony, before the French Academy),[1] Paul Valéry once said something of the word "virtue" that seems to hold true for the word "sin" as well: namely, that the word *vertu* is dead. This observation, he said, one could easily verify simply by noticing how the word appears only in such confined settings as the catechism, operettas . . . and the *Académie Française!*

Yet there is one sphere of discourse – religious language – where one does speak of sin without embarrassment, without having to overcome an inner resistance, as if the matter were quite obvious. Here sin is woven into the very fabric of the ordinary language of the believer. But is that not itself a problem? To hear of sin spoken of so unproblematically in the language of faith and yet so rarely elsewhere prompts one to ask whether such a "disconnect" from everyday language has not itself become the central issue.

Perhaps, though, this contrast is overdrawn. For there is yet another realm we might mention where people use the word "sin" without inhibition or self-consciousness, without a troubled sense that something might be amiss: the entertainment industry. No doubt, in such contexts the word has become trivial and misleading, as in coy expressions like a "night of sin" or a "sinful woman," terms usually spoken with a wink and a nod. Even bishops have been heard to talk this way: for example, the Archbishop of New Orleans welcomed a philosophical convention to his city in early 1968 by saying that, in contrast to New York or Chicago, tourists could walk in the streets of his city at night without anxiety, for here there might be, in his words, "much *sin*, but little *crime*."

To be sure, whether one can say the same thing about "sin," at least by analogy, that Paul Valéry said in his Academy address about the word "virtue" – that the word is for all intents and purposes dead – is more than a little questionable; and for this reason we must continue to pursue our investigation of its usage.

Take, for example, the case of ancient Rome. Linguistic habits in the Late Republic and Early Empire (that is, the Rome of the so-called "classical" period) do not seem to be essentially different from what our linguistic survey has discovered about contemporary usage (namely, that nowadays the word "sin" is used only in confined settings like the catechism, or is ironically meant, as in the entertainment industry, etc.). In a learned philological treatise,[2] for example, one Dutch author claims from his scholarly survey that the religious concept of sin no longer had any vital reality for Romans living in the Golden Age of the Empire. Words denoting sin in Latin (*nefas, piaculum, peccatum, culpa*) had by then become, so the author claims, "museum pieces." What's more, in a remarkable parallel with today, the term *peccatum* was used more often than not in a pointedly ironic sense for misdeeds of a sexual or erotic nature scarcely taken seriously anymore. So the phenomenon we observed at the outset of this essay is nothing specifically "modern." A remarkable similarity, and surely indicative of something pervasive about the human condition.

Still, despite this seemingly uncanny parallel, one cannot really conclude merely from citing the statistics of word usage, either in the case of ancient Rome or in our own time, that the reality denoted by the word "sin" has simply disappeared from man's consciousness and been relegated to a "museum piece." The situation is obviously much more complicated than what it might seem to be at first glance.

In a letter to Gerhart Hauptmann, Thomas Mann captures both the underlying reality and the surface light-heartedness of the term when he apologizes to his older colleague for having portrayed him in a rather dubious light in his novel, *The Magic Mountain*: "I have a guilty conscience and admit I have sinned," he half-confesses. "I say *sinned*," he goes on to say, "because the word has a double dynamic: on the one hand, it is strong and hard, as is quite appropriate to the concept, yet is also, in certain contexts, a half-jovial, familiar and mildly facetious word."[3] These lines are, I think, a sharply perceptive formulation of the semantic range lurking behind the use of the word "sin." Linguistically attuned novelist that he is, Mann captures that range with the delicate sensibility and assured competence of the true poet [*des Dichters*].

Even if the more whimsical, "mildly facetious" surface usage occasionally clouds over and obscures the "strong and hard" meaning, pushing it into the background, nonetheless what has been obscured – and even forgotten – has by no means thereby disappeared from human consciousness. What holds true for all fundamental stances toward existence holds true for sin as well: we know much more than we "know." According to an *obiter dictum* of Friedrich von Hügel[4] the meaning of one's statements doesn't so much depend on what someone *thinks* he means as on what he is *really* thinking.

This is because what "really" is meant by such a basic word as "sin" is generally not just what is *objectively* included, but also the *subjective* connotations implied by the speaker – even if in most cases this connotation is not "realized" or made explicitly present to the speaker's reflective consciousness. Only occasionally will this meaning emerge into the light of day – perhaps without the speaker even realizing how it happened – when a strongly existential tremor brings the hidden depth-dimension of the semantic field into view. The word, until now used only in its superficial sense, spontaneously emerges undiminished into the glaring light of consciousness; and the lips now speak a word, seemingly unbidden, with a fresh content and meaning.

T. S. Eliot has brilliantly depicted a transition of this sort in *The Cocktail Party*: at a crucial moment in the play, the concept of sin suddenly shifts from its dismissive "salon" sense to its true, ultimate core. One might even claim that this shift constitutes the very center (the turning point [*epistrophé*] according to classical theory) of Eliot's unsparing serio-comedy. The plot deals with the figure of the young Celia Coplestone, who in a moment of flashing insight suddenly realizes that an amorous affair she has been pursuing with the husband of another woman (a connection that she had previously found to be entirely fulfilling) has just dissolved into nothing. Or more accurately, she suddenly sees that the relationship has been entirely vain from the very beginning. This unsought yet completely irrefutable insight shakes the life of this young woman down to its foundations.

Quite at a loss and utterly disconcerted, she turns for advice to a physician – who in Eliot's classical plotting functions somewhat like the messenger from higher powers in Greek drama. There's something, she tells the doctor, not quite right:

CELIA: . . . I should really *like* to think there's something wrong
with me –
Because, if there isn't, there's something wrong
Or at least, very different from what it seemed to be,
With the world itself – and that's so much more frightening!
That would be terrible. So I'd rather believe
There is something wrong with me, that could be put right.

She tries to name this disorder. Finally, after a lot of
hemming and hawing, she comes up with the only diagno-
sis that seems to her to specify her symptoms, the unavoidable explanation for her dilemma:

CELIA: It sounds ridiculous – but the only word for it
That I can find, is a sense of sin.
DR. REILLY: You suffer from a sense of sin, Miss Coplestone?
That is most unusual.
CELIA: It seemed to *me* abnormal. . . .
. . . my bringing up was pretty conventional –
I had always been taught to disbelieve in sin.
Oh, I don't mean that it was ever mentioned!
But anything wrong from our point of view,
Was either bad form, or was psychological.
. . . And yet I can't find any other word for it.
It must be some kind of hallucination;
Yet, at the same time, I'm frightened by the fear
That it might be more real than anything I believed in.
REILLY: What is more real than anything you believed in?
CELIA: It's not the feeling of anything I've ever *done*,
Which I might get away from, or of anything in me
I could get rid of – but of emptiness, of failure
Towards someone, or something, outside of myself;
And I feel I must . . . *atone* – is that the word?
Can you treat a patient for such a state of mind?

What is happening here, without flinching words, is that the true and ultimate meaning of the word "sin" – which despite everything has never been forgotten – is now being retrieved from its hidden lair into the clear, reflected presence of consciousness. The reality that up to now had never even been pronounced, indeed not even so much as thought about (precisely because it seems so unthinkable!), now suddenly becomes formulable: namely, that sin is a *warping*, a contortion so twisted and twisting that it must hurl man into total despair, and irrespective of whether this sin can be healed or is entirely "normal." Sin is an inner contortion whose essence is misconstrued if we interpret it as sickness or, to descend into an even more trivializing level, merely as an infraction against conventional rules of behavior.

On the contrary, sin in its reality *means* a failure that has been committed before a superhuman judging power who longs for a reconciliation. But even this sense that reconciliation is required does not really come from the sinner's own consciousness *per se*: this is a reconciliation whose necessity strikes the soul of the sinner with the overpowering evidence of this same judging power – and precisely by giving the sinner insight into the truth of the real content of sin. Experiences of this sort – ones in which the ultimate meaning of the word irresistibly rises up to the recalling power of consciousness – are possible for every one and at all times.

For this reason perhaps it is all for the best that the most ultimate and serious things remain protected from overfamiliarity by our reluctance to bandy about terms for them at any casual moment, a habit that would only turn our experiences of them into shopworn and threadbare clichés.

So we keep silent about them, almost as if we needed to "quarantine" them for hygienic reasons. It might even be that apparently superficial (and even fatuous) chatter about sin means only that we are simply paying homage to the great spiritual leaders and pedagogues of the past, all of whom, of course, took sin extremely seriously but who preferred for the most part to speak of it dismissively [*untertreibend*], saying things like this: "He didn't behave very nobly." "If the proverb is true 'Well begun is half done,' then let's just say he got off to a bad start." "He acted foolishly." "He really blew it" [*daneben gehauen*], and so forth.

On the other hand, perhaps something else more sinister is at play here, something more worrisome, although it might be premature to speak of it in any detail at this stage of the discussion. Still, the matter has already come up in our initial (purely linguistic) circumscription of the word "sin," and so cannot be overlooked even here. An example: Ernst Jünger once called Hitler's order to kill prisoners of war one of his worst "blunders."[5] Yes, the word "blunder" is being used here with a deliberately sardonic iciness. Obviously, it would have been much more literally accurate to speak of a *crime*, of a *monstrous deed*, an outrageous *violation of justice*. Yet even here, we would still hesitate to speak of a "serious sin," a term almost never linked in ordinary discourse with terms like "immense crimes" and the like. In fact we do not just hesitate, we would consider it to be clearly inappropriate, almost impermissible, to use such a term in a context like this. Why? Why such spontaneous, yet completely unreflective bristling whenever someone speaks in the same breath of serious sin and monstrous crime?

I think such bristling means that something known for

a long time – even if it has also been half-forgotten – comes back to mind: namely, the insight that we are in no position to label *any* concrete deed by *any* other person with this name "sin" (needless to say, we are now taking the word in its full, undiminished meaning). For that, a superhuman insight would be required. Of course we fully recognize that "sin," in its fullest meaning, is far more than just a real "possibility" but is completely familiar to post-Adamic, historical man. From the beginning we have known, however inchoately, that human failures at their root can be something much more serious than mere "blunders" or unintentional behavioral patterns. But for those same reasons – despite sin's prevalence and the appropriateness of the word in so many situations – we are also well aware that we should not bandy about the term "sin" in ordinary speech, where it does not quite seem fitting. This is why we so rarely hear the word in ordinary conversation: the word really refers to that place where each human being lives in the innermost secret cell of his person, a place to which no one else has any access whatever.

Clearly, though, it is one thing when people do not explicitly use the term "sin" in their daily rounds and conversations with each other, even though they all readily recognize its real presence in the world [one does not mitigate Hitler's crimes by not applying the term "sin" to them]. It is an entirely *different* thing to deny or ignore its real existence in the technical professional language of critical reflection. Discrete silence is something quite different from the deliberate refusal to speak about what demands our acknowledgment. [*Schweigen ist etwas anders als Verschweigen.*]

But that is just what one does – one refuses to speak as

one is obligated to do – when one tries to give a *purely philosophical explanation* for the concept of sin: meaning, when someone discusses the whole of the world and existence strictly under each of its rationally accessible [*denkbaren*] aspects and eschews insights from any other realm. Such a procedure, however, misses the essential element of the concept of sin. Unfortunately, this blind spot is rarely acknowledged. Whoever, for example, would want to draw wisdom from Rudolph Eisler's three-volume *Wörterbuch der philosophischen Begriffe* [*Dictionary of Philosophical Concepts*] – even if just to get a kind of first, provisional orientation – would not even come across an entry for "sin"! And if our seeker of wisdom were to guess that perhaps something might be learned from Mr. Eisler's entry on "guilt," he would be directed to look up another entry entirely, the one on "accountability" [*Zurechnung*], where finally a few quite meager asseverations could be gleaned.

Not surprisingly, such explicit ignoring of the issue corresponds to a fundamental view of man explicitly espoused in such theories as those encountered in, for example, Nicholai Hartmann and Martin Heidegger. In his *Ethics* (first edition, 1925), easily the most thoroughgoing and normative statement of the genre to appear under so ambitious a title in the last several decades, Hartmann says, for example, that ethics does not know the concept of sin at all: "ethics has no room for sin," the author baldly asserts.[6] In Heidegger's almost simultaneously published *opus magnum*, the epochal *Being and Time*, one also can read that "philosophical questions essentially know nothing of sin."[7]

Of course both authors are familiar with the concept of sin. Hartmann explicitly defines sin as "the same moral guilt of which ethics also speaks, but not 'as' moral guilt, that is, not as guilt before the forum of one's own conscience and its values, but rather as guilt *before God.*"[8] As we have already said above, that is exactly the definition of sin that captures its true essence and is the same traditional definition of sin that one can find in Thomas Aquinas as well as in Kant and Kierkegaard. Aquinas: "The guilty character of sin consists in the fact that it is committed against God."[9] Kant: sin means "trespass of the moral law as divine command."[10] And Kierkegaard: "Human guilt becomes sin when the guilty person knows that he stands before God."[11]

Now for Hartmann and Heidegger (as well as for the whole strain of modern anthropology represented by them) it is thus precisely this element of man's moral failure that has been bracketed off from the purview of the philosopher. Which by their logic means the following: If I keep my gaze on the reality of human existence encountering me under every possible aspect accessible to thought (supposedly the very definition of the philosopher's office!); and if I then try to name that which displays itself before me; then there cannot be the least justification for me to speak of "sin." Yes, I might be able from a philosophical perspective to speak of "behavior offensive to values," even of an "infraction against one's own conscience," I can even speak of "guilt." All of these are possible according this school of philosophy.

But: "a violation of a transhuman norm," "a trespass against a divine command," "sin," that sort of thing simply does *not* come within the field of vision of Empirical Man, no matter how hard he tries, as long as he keeps struggling under the first principles of his epistemology. Consequently, under this epistemological logic, it is unphilosophical to speak of "sin" at all. Such a conclusion is inevitable if one considers the justification that Hartmann adduces for this opinion of his: namely, that philosophical ethics is entirely oriented to affairs of this world here below. He even goes so far as to say that it would be an "ethical distortion, immoral, a betrayal of man," if ethics were to bring into its argument "anything whatever pertaining to heaven on earth, including God Himself."[12] As the author rightly sees, according to Christian conviction "sin [is] the starting point for the work of God, the redemption of man."[13] But for Hartmann ethics must insist on the contrary: the concept of sin should actually be called "an ethical violation of values,"[14] "a moral evil," "the infantilization [*Entmündigung*] and degradation of man," "something that should simply not even exist in the moral sense."[15]

If one considers more closely this argumentation, then what will strike the observer as truly astonishing, indeed as downright unprecedented, is how Hartmann's declarations are on their own terms dogmatic statements *of faith* whose sole purpose is to drive the concept "sin" out of philosophical ethics precisely because of its theological character as "a matter of faith"! Just a few steps further down this path and we can hear, not far off in the distance, Nietzsche's rallying cry: "I strangle the Strangler, who bears the name of Sin."[16] "Believe not in sin!"[17] "Get rid of the concept of sin from the world!"[18]

Of course no one can venture to discuss the theme of sin without presuppositions. But what one can do is to declare one's presuppositions as clearly as possible, along with the "pre-suspicions" [*Voraus-Vermutungen*], the hunches as it were, that lie at the root of one's philosophical presuppositions, and bring them to a formulation – precisely the task that this small book has set for itself.

In the following essay, we shall therefore be operating under two assumptions. First, we shall presuppose that there is in general a *believed* truth beyond the realm of known truth ("known" truth is defined here as truth gained through scientific research and in philosophical reflection), in which a dimension accessible in no other way becomes perceptible and shows itself, a dimension of the one visible reality of world and man [*vor Augen liegenden Realität von Welt und Mensch*]. This presupposition will naturally include the clear admission that there can be theological information about what ultimately happens when a person fails morally.

But that shall not be our only presupposition. We shall also be reckoning with the possibility that this object to be discussed from various perspectives can also be made more deeply and clearly accessible to the efforts of a *philosophical* questioner from the light of that transhuman truth. Such "reckoning with a possibility" might seem at first glance to some to be not especially promising, but this is by no means so. In certain cases a great deal can depend on whether someone considers something "possible" or "excluded" from the outset.

At any rate, this is what I mean to say: I explicitly hold myself open to the possibility that, on the basis of the phenomenon of human guilt or because of what we shall discover to be the "ground" of the phenomenon of guilt, something will manifest itself that at first had not even been suspected, something entirely new.

But now I must speak more concretely. Whoever, as a believer, is convinced that man's rejection of God has provoked such immense historical events in its wake as to constitute the essence of the Mysteries of the Christian faith cannot as a philosopher – that is, as a thinker who considers the content of the term "moral failing" under every possible aspect – possibly be of the opinion that this content has been even provisionally, let alone exhaustively, described by saying that moral failure involves only a violation of a behavioral rule established by man himself (or perhaps by "society") or is a violation of that bloodless abstraction called "values."

Quite the contrary, the philosophical believer must expect that his object will have depths that cannot be plumbed, depths that will both undergird and relativize every formulation of every empirical research finding. In other words, he will be prepared to step into the shadow of mystery by means of that which he is trying to understand: the phenomenon under investigation. Perhaps all he will be able to say at that point is that human interpretation cannot penetrate the reality of "guilt" but must place itself within a more comprehensive truth, however much this truth might itself never be grasped "positively." Perhaps this truth will manifest itself to the philosopher only glancingly, in a negative form: in an extreme inner experience or in isolated data that can scarcely be decoded, the kinds of experiences, for example, that seem to be regularly encountered in the analyses of depth psychology.

But before any more exact discussion can get underway, I want to register my extreme annoyance with Hartmann's statement about the "conflict between guilt and sin."[19] Obviously Hartmann is trying to claim that the issue really is between two separated realms, the one being roughly the "ethical" and other the "religious" sphere. I will not let myself be led astray so easily. It is my hope and expectation that the distinctive feature of sin – the quality of violating a transhuman behavioral rule – will become visible precisely as a human action committed against one's better knowledge. We shall see sin as something that cannot be explained away, as something that in this sense continually confronts our experience.

Therefore, the intimation [*Vermutung*] that will form the decisive presupposition of the present essay claims – to put it as succinctly as possible – that man *simultaneously* infringes against the divinely established norm *by*, in Hartmann's words, becoming guilty "before the forum of his own conscience and of his values."[20] According to the unclouded testimony of human tradition, this is precisely what constitutes the essence of "sin."

II
Missing the Mark

If we try to define the concept of "sin" (or, as Goethe used to say about any verbal definition, "put the word in fetters"), then we immediately notice two semantic fields where the concept is most at home. The broader range of meaning encompasses the whole realm of evil, of what is not good, the bad, the *malum*. Whoever thinks of the word "sin" has at that very moment – or rather, to speak more exactly, before the word ever occurred to him – recognized that something is not "in order" with man: something doesn't quite ring true, things are not quite right with him and his existence, and perhaps even with the world as a whole. The other semantic field, more limited, is that of error-prone *actions*, of human failures, of evil caused by deeds, whether of commission or omission. Every sin is a false step [*Fehlleistung*]; but not every human false step is sin in the strict sense of the word – of course not.

We should recall at this point that both the Latin and the Greek terms for sin (*peccatum, hamartia*: used by the New Testament to characterize exactly what we mean by "sin") originally had a further, *non*-ethical meaning. Perhaps it is neither surprising nor remarkable that, in the hundred times Homer uses the verb *hamartanein* to describe a simple action, he is referring to the fact that a warrior hurling his spear has failed to hit his target.[1]

But also in Aristotle, the noun *hamartia* and the verb *hamartanein* are clearly used, on average, much more often to indicate some non-ethical meaning of "missing the mark," such as the diagnostic lapses of a physician, grammatical errors of syntax, slips of the pen, and the like,[2] even though in the *Nicomachean Ethics* the same word usually refers to moral failings. As I say, perhaps none of this will come as a surprise to the reader.

Yet I suspect the same will not be the case if the reader is told that the Bible too (or at any rate the Hebrew of the Old Testament) knows a non-ethical meaning for the word "to sin": to miss the mark. Gerhard Kittel's famous *Theological Dictionary of the New Testament*, on which I rely here, makes the remark that this semantic application of the word to mean "miss the mark" cannot be understood as arising "either from the realm of religious language or from legal or ethical usage," but is actually the historical "basis" for his claim that the *non*-ethical and *non*-religious meaning of the word was the original one.[3]

This etymological history highlights an important feature of the term, one that might not be so obvious in the German [or English] word "sin" as it seems to be even in the Latin term *peccatum*. A writer like Thomas Aquinas, for example, can still revert to the more general meaning of the concept *peccatum*, one that transcends the ethical and religious connotations of the term, however much that means that he is, at least to some extent, pitting himself over against the theological usage of his time. So for example he will say: "Every action that is not in right order can be called *peccatum*, whether it belongs to the realm of nature, art, or morality."[4] And by the term "realm of art," as quickly becomes evident from the context, Aquinas is referring (this time according to standard medieval diction) to every form of production and manufacture, the "technical crafts" in the widest sense of that word as well as those arts "inspired by the muses."

Peccatum means here every kind of false step [*Fehlleistung*], whether that be the engineering mistakes of a bridge-builder, the false notes by the player of a musical instrument, and of course the specifically moral lapses. Wherever there is acting and doing, then there lurks the possibility of false steps, *peccata*. Seen from this point of view, not only can an animal commit a *peccatum* insofar as it "does wrong," but also whenever a fetus is malformed in the womb, even this can be described as a *peccatum naturae*, a false step by nature.[5]

Now it is important to realize that the second, narrower semantic "swatch" of the word "sin" (in the strict sense) is only cut from the cloth of this more comprehensive meaning of *peccatum*, which refers to any false step of causing wrong when the act of doing or making misfires. Thomas uses for this narrower sense (as long as he is using *peccatum* in its generic meaning) the word *culpa*, fault, guilt: "These three things – *malum, peccatum, culpa* – form a kind of declension," he says, "moving from the more to the less general."[6] As we have already seen, Thomas knows quite well that by his own time "*peccatum* and *culpa* are understood in theological discourse as meaning the same thing."[7] But for him something more important was at stake. By going back to a linguistic usage that had already been falling into neglect, he was promising a more penetrating account of the concept of sin, which for him was of course the whole purpose of his disputation. It will therefore perhaps be worthwhile, *before* discussing moral lapses, that is, before taking up the issue of *culpa* – "sin" in the strict sense of the word –, to treat the more general concept of failure, of misfire as such, that is, of *peccatum* in the original sense of the word.

The answer to the question where precisely the failure is located in a false step seems at first glance easily ascertained. A marksman fails to hit the target he is aiming at. What else could be meant here by "false" than this fact: the marksman did not hit the bull's-eye? Now every good shooting instructor can train a novice rifleman to shoot better, in the sense of more accurately. But whenever we are speaking strictly of a true *ability* to shoot, when, that is, we are speaking of the "art" of shooting,[8] then obviously this "art" of shooting is not a matter of the simple fact of happening to strike something. Everyone knows that a person, purely as a matter of beginner's luck, can attain to "marksman" status without knowing the least about the art of shooting. In such cases the shooting instructor can rightly conclude that his pupil has in fact failed to hit the mark, indeed made a gross error, even though the pupil happened to hit the bull's-eye! Such accidental hits can rightly be characterized as a *peccatum* because – like the "gang that couldn't shoot straight" but occasionally hit the mark – the neophyte has violated the *norms* for good marksmanship. There is a wonderful story that Eugen Herrigel tells in his popular book, *Zen in the Art of Archery*,[9] about an old Japanese Zen master. The master is teaching the art of archery to a Western novice, and he reacts quite angrily to a behavior that he regards as quite dishonorable and deceptive. For the novice, after years of training, has learned only how to release the arrow abruptly, albeit "correctly," from his hand. All the novice wants is to foreshorten the time he has to spend in training; so he exploits a trick that happens to be "successful" but which goes contrary to the Zen master's rules.

Astonishingly enough, Thomas Aquinas says exactly the same thing, naturally not of archery specifically but in a general sort of way and of course with man's moral failings in view: "Not to observe the rules of action belongs more essentially to the concept of the misdirected step than does the failure to reach the goal."[10] To formulate this insight more pointedly,[11] one might even say: what makes a bad shot bad is not so much that one has missed the target as that one has violated the rules of marksmanship. Of course, it is still true that the whole point of marksmanship is to hit the bull's-eye. The rules of shooting have their justification only because they make hitting the target that much more probable – *not* as happenstance, but as something to be expected "as a rule," precisely because one is following the rule.

The *goal* of action, the *rules* of action: these two obviously belong together: the norm of action is not to be thought of as an isolated regulation established without any bearing on the goal. On the contrary, what a norm "should" do is order and structure the activity according to a plan for reaching the goal, the rule being meant to subserve the aimed-for goal. This connection is precisely what justifies our thesis that seemed paradoxical at first glance: that what is "most essentially" false in a false step is not the fact that one has missed the mark but rather that one has not observed the norms of action.

On the other hand, as we have already indicated, we have clearly still not "hit upon," so to speak, what makes sin sinful when we call it a false *step* [*Leistung*], even though it is most definitely something bad manifested in a *deed*. The main difference – or more exactly, one of the differences – lies in the willingness, the acquiescence of one's will, that is, in the *voluntarium*.[12] It belongs to the nature of moral failings to be freely willed, while all other kinds of false steps are, without exception, unwilled. They all happen, as it were, inadvertently [*unversehentlich*], for which reason one cannot, on their account, become either guilty or be held responsible for them, since they are essentially "technical" errors [*Kunstfehler*]. *Artifex non culpatur*: the artist, artificer, or craftsman cannot, as a human being, be made guilty for what he has made poorly: clumsiness is no sin.[13]

One might perhaps object at this point: should not, for example, a physician justifiably be held responsible in tort law for a "technical" failure in his craft? Here I would say: the activity of a doctor is no "pure case," because obviously it does not take place in a discipline determined solely by pure technique, of what is right or wrong from a strictly technical point of view. The technical competence of a physician also ineluctably affects how the doctor is respecting or harming the patient to whom he has solemnly pledged to do his best: *primum non nocere*, first do no harm, says the Hippocratic Oath. Thus a deficiency in medical skill, although it cannot "in itself" be accounted to the doctor as his fault, in fact must count, at the very least, as a negligent violation against the moral norm of human sociality [*Mitmenschlichkeit*], which clearly involves a matter of justice. Of course the counter-example is also conceivable: can there really be a "pure case" of a false step that is nothing but a technical failure?

First of all, we have yet to test our previous assertion: does it in fact belong to the concept of a false step – with the lone exception of moral lapses – to be unwilled, unintentional, inadvertent? Ordinary language, in my opinion, gives a completely clear answer. No one, for example, can intentionally make an arithmetic mistake. Anyone who knowingly adds his sums incorrectly in his tax forms and then, to excuse himself, says he "made a mistake in his sums" is lying. Even the teacher who deliberately slips in an error when writing out an example of sums on the blackboard as a cunning way of testing the skills or attention span of slow or drowsy pupils is, as everyone would admit, not making a "mistake." The teacher's procedure here in entirely correct – in view of the ultimate goal of making his pupils think out the answer on their own – a goal the instructor obviously thinks is more important than providing the nominally "correct" sum.

Such a deliberate introduction of error in the context of a more comprehensive goal can, when a good reason prompts the intention, happen with every trespass against a "rule of craft," that is, with every non-ethical false step. But it is *never* possible, in principle, when we are dealing with the case of a moral lapse or of any moral action whatever. Why? Because there simply *is* no more "important" context transcending the moral! Marksmanship, arithmetic, painting, treating wounds – all of these activities can rightly be subordinated to a greater goal in the course of accomplishing that goal. But that is simply not possible for ethical action in the strict sense.

As Thomas Aquinas says, there are two points above all that distinguish the *peccatum in actu artis* ("technical failure," in other words) from moral failings, from what he calls *peccatum in moralibus*.[14] First, every exercise in art (in the widest sense of that word, including all forms of craftsmanship) is ordered to a goal that is not the goal of existence as a whole. The goal that the arts have set for themselves is always particular. Thus the "craftsman's *mistake*," in contrast to a moral failing, consistently affects only a partial goal, never the goal of life itself.

Second, man sets for himself the goals of training in the arts and crafts; they are something "contrived by human reason" [*durch die menschliche Vernunft Ausgedachtes*]. A "failure in technique" – as opposed to a moral failing – never violates the goals given with the very existence and nature of man, ends which we have already discovered with our very existence itself, ends established by a higher, more powerful and overarching perfection.

Admittedly, one reads with a certain uneasiness this assertion that the ends of art deal merely with "something contrived by man." Such a way of putting things makes the arts sound like adventitious, extraneous additions to human activity. Can such a formulation really apply to great literature and music? But before the reader protests, one should recall that the ancients understood by the term "art" (*ars*) not just the finished quality of what was being fashioned, the *recta ratio factibilium*, such as a sonnet or a passacaglia, but also the instruments for their realization, or any ordinary artifact, such as a violin or a lock on a door. The hushed tones in which the word "art" is nowadays pronounced with an almost religious devotion were utterly unknown to the ancients, from Aristotle to Johann Sebastian Bach.[15] Quite the contrary, they soberly insisted that every artistic exercise, whether technical or one inspired by the Muses, is a *human* activity, and that all works of art are *human* works (at least human works *as well*), proceeding from human design and springing up from man's own goals that he had previously set for himself.

Perhaps we should reintroduce here the example of the

so-called "medical arts" and recall that their goal, the healing of the sick, can scarcely be called simply "something contrived by human reason." That sounds plausible, no doubt. Still, it is the human being himself who, as a doctor, must decide on his own whether a medical intervention is called for or how an operation should proceed. And beyond that, it also is a matter of personal decision whether he is going to become a doctor rather than, say, a teacher, architect, musician. No one violates a strictly obligatory requirement by preferring another profession, even if there seems to be evidence, perhaps even a "vocation," of medical talent in the individual that would strongly direct him or her to that profession.

The same applies to all fields: healing, teaching, construction, musicianship. They are all life-forms and careers by which human beings set goals for themselves and which all clearly go back to some aboriginating human decision, whereas *being* human is no more a matter of decision than is the end of human existence itself. Here we have no choice, no decision to make, nor is there anything here for our reason "to contrive." Rather, we find this prior determination of the goal as something already set for us, without our having been consulted in the matter, just as we find ourselves already existing in the world, precisely as *these* beings who have been fashioned in *this* way. Now if things are to go aright, every particular, self-chosen goal must be subordinated and connected to this end of existence as a whole, and that would include every conceivable artistic activity, whether that be the art of the doctor or of the poet.

Presumably, then, there is no such thing, seen as a whole, as a *purely* technical problem (medical, literary, manufacturing, and so forth) that can be solved and overcome exclusively on the basis of the criteria of mere craftsmanship [*Kunstübung*]. No artistic skill is conceivable that could take place outside of human existence; all production of works, all manufacture of objects (*facere, poiein*), is unavoidably and at the same time human action, doing (*agere, praxis*).

Because that is so, it is easy to establish from the nature of the case that there can always be two kinds of lapses when we are speaking of manufacture, in other words of "art" in the wider sense, craftsmanship. The *first* possibility of making a false step is an "artistic error" in the strict sense, that is, the failure to get "just right" whatever goal the artist has in mind: the marksman fails to hit the bull's-eye, the surgeon nicks an organ essential for life, the engineer's calculations of a bridge's tensile strength prove to be wrong. The *second* ever-present possibility for making a false step in the realm of art and manufacture consists in the dilemma that one might reach the goal set for oneself, perhaps brilliantly, but at the same time, *for that same reason*, will have violated the universal goal of existence as a whole.

This distinction provides us with one of the truly indispensable tools for clarifying the question of this essay. Without it, we could never sufficiently explain, or even discuss, the responsibility of the "arts" for the common good. To link an artist's "misfiring" with moral lapses, at least conceptually (in the manner of our second possibility), implies that the "technical" arts are just as important as the "Muses'" arts (recall the older, more encompassing concept of *artes*). For the methods and procedures of medicine, politics, advertising, manufacture and commerce, and so forth, all have obvious ethical implications, and precisely at the moment when, and insofar as, they reach their art-specific goals.

One need only think of the development and production of nuclear weapons: obviously *their* manufacture must be subordinated to norms other than the rules of engineering [*Kunstregeln*], rules that can only dictate making such weapons as technically perfect as possible. Here surely is a situation where the standard that something be "technically sweet" is utterly irrelevant. This must be clear by now to the entire world! (As is well known, this was how J. Robert Oppenheimer characterized the way experimental physicists had let themselves get seduced: they were tempted into thinking that building an atom bomb was in fact feasible because of the engineering simplicity of the mechanism, an intimation of its technical beauty that was directly linked with the first inklings of its feasibility.[16])

Obviously here – if anywhere! – we are not dealing with a "merely" technical problem. In this context there can be no question of a pure instance of "art," that is, of how one can go about making an artifact or contraption like this. Rather, a project like this can be assessed and undertaken, *if at all*, only after first considering the historical existence of man as a whole and the goals and ends entailed in being human.

But then, that same consideration must basically hold true for *all* forms of human activity in which a particular goal is set and realized according to definite rules of technique and "art." Such "arts" are always subject not only to procedural norms, but also simultaneously to a norm that transcends them, one that binds man not simply as an artist, technician, expert, but as a *persona humana* – a norm that has from time immemorial been called a "moral" norm.

Naturally, the issue might be extremely hard to judge in the concrete case; we could hardly expect otherwise. But whoever does not accept and take into consideration this decisive distinction between the two kinds of possible failings in artistic-technical activity (however much it might at first seem a pedantic one) is simply not equipped even to perceive the problem inherent to human action, let alone solve it. For example, if someone says, as one is constantly hearing and reading these days from influential critics and writers of *haute littérature*, that there are only well and poorly written books but no good or bad ones,[17] then naturally it is a hopeless enterprise from the outset to discuss with him whether a particular book might corrupt the reader, lead to licentiousness, and so forth.

Nor should we think this to be a specifically "Christian" theme. Representatives of both points of view have been represented in the European intellectual tradition for at least two thousand years. I know, for example, of an author who holds that "what one thinks and writes is completely a matter of indifference." He expresses himself on the issue so strongly and apodictically that the conviction has clearly become second nature to him. And how modern it sounds! As it happens, this manifesto comes from an important modern German novelist; yet Plato has the sophist Gorgias say almost the same thing: what is decisive is not the subject matter [*Gegenstand*] an artist chooses, but for Gorgias how it is depicted, the style, the form, the diction.

Nor is the contrary thesis specifically Christian either, for Plato demands not only that everyone else but he too – Plato himself, with his extremely delicate sensibility for literary style! – hold to just this thesis: something might be well made, perfectly said, charmingly formulated, and still, when looked at from the perspective of the whole and of what really counts, can be false and deeply vicious.

Needless to say, examples of the disparity are legion. The shot that killed Martin Luther King was no doubt, when considered from a purely technical point of view, a brilliantly executed "direct hit." But the first-class marksman was also, and by that very fact, a murderer. A surgical intervention might well be both a criminal abortion and an extraordinarily well done, "successful" operation. *Artifex non culpatur*.[18] The marksman and surgeon, insofar as they have mastered and now possess the techniques of their trade, are rather to be praised than accused. Yet as assassin or abortionist – that is, when we consider both men as moral persons, or as Thomas says, *inquantum sunt homines*[19] – their failings [*Fehlleistungen*] are glaring.

At this point we must radicalize the sentence quoted above (which was in any event already quite problematic) about the "innocence of art," a view which seems to be so distinctively modern. Certainly, contemporary society, organized around the principle of the division of labor, favors the view that "*action* can be transposed to a morally neutral perspective by the simple expedient of applying instead the term *labor*."[20] And so "labor" – which of itself "reeks" no more than money does (*non olet*, as the scholastics used to say) – can become the "camouflage for action."[21] That is, one can disengage a purely technical artifact [*Verrichtung*] belonging to the realm of the *artes* from the total context of morality by concentrating solely on the labor that went into it. By its very nature, a moral action is oriented to the meaning of existence as a whole; but when "activity" becomes "labor," then a person can claim he is "only doing his job." As long as the work is, as we say, a "job well done," everything seems in order. Not even one's humanity seems to be at risk.

In his autobiography, the last *Kommandant* of

Auschwitz portrayed the functioning of his annihilation camp as an enormous organizational accomplishment. From the precisely worked-out timetable of the Transportation Ministry to the carefully calibrated capacity of the crematoria, with their "incinerating possibilities" developed to the maximum – none of this escapes his attention.[22] The inventor of napalm, when confronted with photographs of burn victims, said that he understood his task as a "purely scientific challenge in Research and Development," one which he would gladly assume all over again.[23]

As a brief summary of all that has been said above, we can list the results of our analysis in the following five points:

1. Sin is a human *doing*, an *act* of man; and thus not primarily a *condition*, although use of the word to describe a condition is not unknown. For example in the New Testament, especially in John, we encounter such statements as this: "If you were blind, you would have no sin" (John 9:41). Here sin seems to resemble a disease, something one "has," like leprosy. Or when Paul says, "dead to sin but alive to God" (Romans 6:11), he seems to be speaking of sin as a power conceived in almost personal terms. In fact the earliest mention of the concept of "sin" in the Bible ("If you do not do what is right, sin is crouching at your door," Genesis 4:7) must be interpreted in just such a sense. Martin Buber says the biblical word for "sin" can be translated in contemporary language only "glancingly." In his own translation of the Hebrew Scriptures, for example, he suggests the word *Lagerer* (highwayman) for "sin," rather as if sin were lurking before the castle gates like some demonic bandit.[24]

The attempt to define the entire realm encompassed by

the word "sin" can hardly dispense with bringing this whole semantic range into consideration, although the starting point must still remain the fact that "sin" primary is a *doing*, a human deed. "Sin is not simply a deficiency, it is an *act* [deficient in the sense that it lacks the requisite ordering]."[25] "Being ordered to a goal happens by doing; sin consists in this, it disturbs the ordering toward the goal, essentially in a doing."[26]

2. Although sin is a disturbance in one's ordered orientation to one's end, it is also at the same time, and perhaps beforehand, an infringement against a behavioral rule. Such a rule is naturally not to be thought as a context-free, positivistic "arrangement" that might have been otherwise, but rather as a directional pointer to the end to be attained, an end already given with the meaning of the doing itself. As a consequence the injury done to the norm simultaneously makes reaching the goal something unlikely and accidental.

3. We are not the ones who determine the end or goal. Failure to reach this goal is the essence of sin, but it is not for us to choose what that goal will be in the first place, as if by some arbitrary choice. On the contrary, we already find ourselves oriented toward this end without having been consulted about the matter. Here we are *not* free. Admittedly, many thinkers (Jean-Paul Sartre, for example) hold the opposite and claim that even the very possibility of existing as a human being at all, and with such-and-such a nature, must be decided upon. To which Thomas gives the tart reply: "The requirement of determining the ultimate end is not among those things of which we are masters."[27]

4. Because this goal entailed in the nature of man himself obviously intends to include the whole of human being [*Dasein*], not to attain that goal necessarily also affects and distorts the core of his existence. No other conceivable type of false step could make man guilty except moral failing: that is, sin. It alone disturbs or corrupts the inner movement of man toward his deepest and most fitting end. A technical or artistic failure can indeed make the work "bad," but never the artist (or apprentice) as a person, whereas moral failings do make man "evil," pure and simple.[28]

5. "In the full sense of the word that act is moral that stands entirely and completely in our power."[29] Which means: it also belongs to the concept of moral failure, and thus of sin itself, that one must be responsible and accountable for it. If this freedom to decide (by virtue of which we are able to affirm or deny the goal already pre-established with our nature and existence) is lacking; if the false step or lapse committed by us does not lie directly in our power, willed by us and welling up "within us," *in nobis*,[30] in our very selves; – then there is also neither guilt nor sin in the strict sense.

In the discussion thus far we have not yet explicitly treated the idea of moral failure presupposed at the outset of this essay – namely, that sin is in the last analysis an infringement against a transhuman, absolute norm, is resistance against God Himself. But we have at least glimpsed an immense reality so unsettling that thought about man can scarcely ever do justice to it. We now know that man is faced with an ominously stark possibility: he can, of his

THE CONCEPT OF SIN

own free will, fail to reach the goal and meaning of his existence as a whole.

Given the immensity of this possibility and given everything that rides on it (which really *is* everything!), there is certainly nothing easier to comprehend than the perennial attempt to interpret and explain away this extremely unsettling thought: how could man possibly deny so fundamentally the fundamentals of his existence?

This possibility at first seems so muddled and inconsistent that is typically dispatched by one of two methods. One can either deny, or at least mitigate, the willingness to sin by saying that the allegedly or only apparently guilty person is actually someone who doesn't know what he is doing. In other words, the guilty person has gone astray, has been "blinded," perhaps even been driven by the Godhead into the darkness. (The fearsome ancient concept of *até*, of a fate decreed by Zeus but still a fate for which man is accountable, fits here as part of this type of strategy.)

But the question put by Plato's Socrates should be recalled here: doesn't virtue ultimately rest on insight, and so aren't all guilty deeds actually done out of ignorance? To this rather rhetorical question Søren Kierkegaard had the right answer: If sin is ignorance, then there is no sin, since sin includes by definition the notion of 'conscious intent.'"[31] Another of these literally exculpatory strategies comes from the Jesuit paleontologist Teilhard de Chardin, who tried to explain sin as a kind of "statistical necessity": wherever a plurality is trying to organize itself into a unity, there will necessarily be a certain frequency of mistakes. For example, with mass mailings some letters are bound to get through without a stamp, others will be misaddressed and yet get through, others will be correctly franked and addressed and never arrive, and so forth. But as with Socrates, this strategy only succeeds by ignoring the crux of the issue, in this case the intentionality of moral lapses.[32] By its very nature sin cannot be an inadvertent mistake [*Versehen:* an overlooking of something]. Unwilled lapse is never sin.

The second way of dismissing the immensity entailed by the concept of sin comes from Nietzsche, who did not try to deprive sin of its willed character but sought instead to deny it had the quality of evil! "I rejoice in great sin as my great consolation."[33]

Even so, no one has ever been able to shake off the conviction that it belongs to the possibility of historical man to fail to attain, of his own free will, the goal that constitutes the very meaning of life. No one has ever been able to argue himself out of the conviction that man is in fact a being of such a kind (perhaps one should say: of such a rank) that he can become guilty in the full, unattenuated sense and with all its consequences in mind.

But how can we ever explain or make plausible to ourselves this frightening thought? How could a human being possibly and with full deliberateness undertake an act of resistance to the very meaning of his own existence? It would be premature at this juncture of the discussion to discuss this question formally. Yet, as a question explicitly posed and deliberately left hanging, it is meant to determine the atmosphere and tone of the following reflections.

III
Contra Naturam, Contra Rationem

It is not just a figure of speech to say that when sin happens something is "not in order." Ordinary expressions like "contrary to good order" and "disordered" are phrases that have been linked ("ordered," if you will) to the concept of sin from the very beginnings of philosophical and theological reflection, and in several senses. Sin is a disordered act,[1] but not just sin. The claim is that the soul, too, falls into disorder because of sin: sin consists in the fact that "the soul has lost her order."[2] St. Thomas speaks as well of the "disordered love of man for himself,"[3] a love which includes as part of its disorder an element of "disordered fear,"[4] which is the case for every sin.

But what does this mean more exactly? What do we intend to say when we claim something is "not in order"? What does that word "order" mean? Let us assume that we are not speaking of administrative order or, still less, of what the police mean by keeping order, as in the expression "law and order." In those two contexts, we are thinking of something static, of a "persistent condition" with this or that configuration. In the great intellectual tradition of Europe, however, the word "order" always referred to something dynamic, as in the Latin phrases that crop up so frequently in legal codes and in medieval thought: *Ordo ad alterum, ordo ad invicem, ordo ad finem* [being ordered to the other, to one another, to a goal]. These verbal linkages are quite common in the Latin tradition, as rich in meaning as the German term *Hin-Ordnung* [order toward].

These telic versions of the term *ordo* imply that right order, in the world at large as well as in the world of human beings, only comes about in the course of *events*, namely, in a dynamic inherent in ourselves that leads in a definite direction appropriate to that dynamic. On the other hand, everything that falls outside this movement-toward is considered disordered, contrary to order. Sin therefore establishes itself as a pointless, literally *relation-less*[5] activity in the special sense: sin lacks the element of being ordered to a goal.

Admittedly, this way of putting the issue sounds rather formalistic. But the picture changes as soon as we add some other characteristics to the portrait, features that theologians of the first Christian millennium from Augustine to Thomas sought to link to the concept of sin.[6]

Let us begin with St. Thomas's principle that "every sin is contrary to nature."[7] Notice that what is meant here by *contra naturam* is something quite general: *every* sin (and not just, for example, those sexual sins called "unnatural" in the penal codes) is understood not just as a violation of the nature of man himself but even more of the natural order as a whole.[8] Of course this immediately raises the question of how, and on what basis, the concept of "nature" might be understood to contain an element of direction, obligation, or even duty. But however we go about answering that question, this much at least is clear: in the idea of "order" the general contours of such teleological elements are clearly recognizable.

At this point we cannot fail to mention a crucial insight,

one so fundamental that it serves as the foundation for all traditional teaching about the good life. Prior to the rise of modernity everyone shared the common conviction that the first and most decisive standard for determining norms of conduct in the whole realm of human action must be *nature*: what man and things are "by nature" is what determines norms for good and evil. Moreover, the phrase "by nature" basically meant: by virtue of having been created, by virtue of one's being a creature. In other words, man's "nature" can virtually be identified with his creaturely status: his being a creature – his coming into the world without his consent – defines his innermost essence. Everything, therefore, that man can do as a self-aware, consciously deciding essence is based on, and necessarily already presupposed by, what he is by nature. And here "nature" means not just the earliest and first genetic endowment (nature in the sense of "by birth") but also the permanent norm.

Human knowledge is thus true only when it is founded on what we know naturally [*naturhaft*]. Above all, those activities of man that proceed from free decision and choice are good only when they put into action what our wills have already willed from the beginning by their nature. Of course as the word itself implies, "human nature" refers to what comes with being born [*natus, natura*], which we can neither choose nor make (nor even corrupt). But "nature" also implies growth, which means that we are born not as static entities but as unfinished products, a "rough draft" [*Entwurf*] whose realization is demanded by that same nature "by virtue of creation."[9]

Accordingly, that which man "should" become – that is, the good – is not something arbitrarily spun out and invented, not something unrelated to man's innate essence or to the nature of the things he must deal with. The good, on the contrary, is that final end toward which all his natural drive aims to find articulation and fulfillment. Yet for that very reason evil is not something that should be thought of as somehow separate from that same pregiven ontic condition. Sin is neither something concocted by a "vengeful" God, and nor was it maliciously devised to serve as a leash or a horse's bridle by some kind of moralistic institution. No: "To sin is nothing else but to hang back from the good that belongs to one by nature."[10]

In the context of these remarks, the original meaning of a long-misunderstood term seems almost of its own accord to regain its relevance, a sense that, ever since Kant's well-known denigration of desire as inherently antithetical to duty, has taken on an almost sinister or philistine connotation. I am referring of course to the concept of the *inclinatio naturalis*, the "inclination of nature."[11] Needless to say, this term does not refer to the merely accidental, capricious, grasping wish to get a hold of something, for which the word "appetite" serves. Presumably the "inclination of nature" should be understood (and it will be so understood here) not as referring to anything that can be encountered empirically or psychologically. Rather, the inclination of nature is the hidden gravitational pull that is active in each individual regulation of the will. It is the fundamental energy by virtue of which human existence presses toward its intended goal. The good of the natural inclination is the goal given with it by creation, fed from the originating act of creation, which can itself be thought of in no other way than as an absolutely original explosion from which every creaturely dynamic in the world receives its first impulse and from which it is ever after held in process. Whoever reflects on this and accepts it can scarcely find surprising a

sentence like the following, one that would have been completely taken for granted by all the ancient teachers of wisdom: "Everything that fights against the inclination of
nature is sin."[12]

But suddenly we also encounter another surprise, yet
one entirely conceivable at this juncture of the argument:
namely, the fact that (and the explanation for the fact that)
we never can sin with the unreserved power of our will,
never without an inner reservation, never with one's whole
heart. Because sin always takes place by going against the
natural [*naturhaften*] impulse of the sinner himself, whoever does wrong can never therefore be completely at one
with himself. Even the torments of the damned arise, in the
final analysis, from a dichotomy inside the person: the pain
of being cut off from what the sinner continues to will and
to love by virtue of his very nature.

To be entirely and completely in harmony [*d'accord*]
with oneself – that only occurs to the one who is doing the
good; to him alone belongs that happiness that comes to
the one who is able to throw himself absolutely and with
full sails into what he is doing. As Kierkegaard saw, the
Bible praises "purity of heart" for just this reason. As the
very title of his meditation indicates, the evangelical coun-
sel of "purity of heart" can be realized only in total undi-
videdness and freedom from distraction: "If a human being
is to will the One, then he must will the Good,"[13] for "purity of heart is to will one thing."[14]

Thus, whoever understands "human nature" as a creaturely project [*Entwurf*], already given as innate endowment and yet still waiting to be realized, will immediately
see the answer to our fundamental question, precisely
because he already knows that the concept "nature" contains within itself an element of binding directedness

[*verbindlicher Richtweisung*]. He will already regard as plausible our initial supposition: that a formal lapse [*Verfehlung*] against nature is at the same time and for that reason an infringement against a superhuman norm and thus is guilt before God the Creator.

To be sure, there is not just *one* way to break out of the bonds of this natural orderedness toward a goal that is an inherent part of being a creature. Atheism, whether openly confessed or implicitly held, certainly constitutes one form of this rebellion. By definition, that is, by its very stance, atheism denies or ignores the creatureliness and thus also the provisionality [*Entwurfscharakter*] of the world and man – with the consequence that atheists must explain man's moral failure as, at most, inappropriate behavior, or perhaps as an error of judgment, or, even more tepidly, as an inability to adapt to society.

But there are *theological* forms of this denial as well. One need only think of those ethereal, disconnected theologies which hold that what man is "by nature" (by virtue of his creatureliness) is unimportant and in any event non-binding for ethics. But that only means that man's well-being, as well as his sin, seem to be separated off from his natural (innate) reality given at birth.

I am scarcely inventing a straw-man here. In fact, I would go so far as to say that the decisive mark of certain modern theologians is precisely this "great divorce" between man's nature and his ethical presuppositions. The Marxist observer of the Christian scene, Roger Garaudy, has by no means got his facts wrong when he openly praises contemporary Christian theology for having attained, in his opinion, the maturity of self-determination. According to his interpretation, human existence now comes across to theology above all as man's liberation from his own nature,

THE CONCEPT OF SIN

effected by the grace of Christ![15] But – and here is the rub – this liberation is purchased solely to facilitate a decision completely severed from any connection with a predetermined goal, solely to be completely open to the future as a blank slate.

What else can explain the almost exclusive obsession with the future, with the theme of hope, in so much contemporary theology? What else but this kind of non-teleological existential philosophy lurks behind the relentless focus on the future as a blank slate, as if nothing has been pregiven as part of our creatureliness, that is, as part of what man is "by nature"? How I would hate to be regarded as a "theologian" if that is what the word meant! In fact, in a public disputation with Jürgen Moltmann in 1967,[16] I allowed as how I would be deeply upset and would have to reconsider my own position, regarding everything I had held in the past with deep distrust, if I, as a Christian theologian, were to find myself being interpreted in the same way that so intelligent a critic as Roger Garaudy has done with others. My partner in disputation – next to Karl Barth perhaps the most influential Protestant theologian since the end of the Second World War – then replied that he completely agreed with Garaudy's interpretation and wanted to be accounted among those the Marxist praised! Moltmann, too, was completely convinced that Christian existence begins *ex nihilo*!

This position is, it seems to me, demonstrably false. In reality *everything* that we do of our own responsibility, whether or not we are Christians, can be set into motion *at all* only on the basis of this fundamental presupposition: that both world and man are beings called into existence by virtue of their creatureliness. Moreover, from just that same presupposition – our reality as creatures – we are presented with the standard, the boundary, the norm for our decisions, decisions which are *not* drawn "from nothing," but are decisions *of* the creature, *as* a creature.

It is inadmissible to think that man's moral failings [*sittliche Fehlleistung*] can be swept into some isolated, cordoned-off realm of "grace" and "interiority." Rather "guilt before God" simultaneously concretizes itself as a violation against what world and man are "because of creation" – which is why it is completely legitimate to say that every sin is "against nature."

If, as is my hope, all of these connections have, at least to some extent, become clear and plausible to the reader, then I must muddy the waters once more so that the whole complexity of the subject matter can stay in the foreground. After all, the subject matter of this essay is not just complex and multifaceted. It is even more – a *mysterium*.

Now traditional Christian anthropology not only makes the claim that sin *contradicts* what we naturally want but also, strangest of all, is *founded* on what we want: "Every sin is rooted in a natural appetite."[17]

How can that be? Is this not a contradiction? One could say, falling back on the analogy used earlier, that missing the bull's-eye in archery could not even happen if the bow did not have a certain tensile strength and if there were no exertion applied by the archer aiming at the target when he let loose his arrow. Yes, one could concede that point, if only it did not obscure the whole reason for the analogy, precisely because at this moment of the argument the analogy cannot express the central difference between moral and technical failure: namely, that a *moral* lapse is specifically a willed and intentional missing of the mark. And yet, how is this intentionality simultaneously supposed to spring up from the *natural* will or be grounded in it if intentional sin also stands in contradiction to it?

It almost seems as if the fundamental question provoked by this theme – that is, how can sin be conceived as something even humanly possible, given the way the intellect is ordered to the natural will? – has now become both all the more urgent and yet also still more difficult to answer, especially when we try to take all its dimensions into account.

Before we try to tackle that issue, however, we must still consider the third characteristic of sin (a trait that can be found asserted countless times in the tradition): namely, that sin is something contrary to reason, an *actus contra rationem*,[18] a kind of "craziness." Yet despite that, sin is not something diseased, certainly not a "disease" in the ordinary sense of what people mean by that word: something that simply comes upon a person without any choice in the matter. On the contrary, sin goes contrary to reason by a deliberate act committed with full and clear understanding of what one is doing and with full responsibility (which is precisely what makes sin, as people say, that much "*crazier*"!).

Quite spontaneously the concept of "blinding" enters the discussion here, but obviously not in the sense that people mean when they speak of blindness as an *inability* to see, the sheer absence of knowledge, etc. Rather, as we see in common proverbs like "none so blind as those who will not see," the notion of sin's blinding effects includes a dimension of accountability and guilt. Once again we are hit with the weirdness of it all: we get an inkling of an inner contradiction in sin, we feel its absurdity.

Even the intensely rational neo-Platonic mystic who hid himself under the name of Dionysius the Areopagite called evil *alogon* [the irrational].[19] And that famous "Aristotelian" Thomas Aquinas appeals to the Areopagite for his thesis that what constitutes sin as sin is exactly this: that sin is contrary to reason.[20] (We should recall that *ratio* means much more than just the ability to reason with logical consistency; it embraces the very essence of man, who is the "rational animal" in every aspect of his being.)

Still, there is no getting around the central dilemma: the conflict between sin and knowledge. Knowledge, however, means illumination of reality, truth, light. Human action is good by virtue of its capacity to adapt to reality, which means that the goodness of action can arise only from its knowledge of reality. But sin contradicts what man knows and sees; it is the denial of the light of reason. "Wherefore, whatever is against this light is for man evil and contrary to his nature."[21]

It would be worth our while to spend a moment reflecting more exactly on this metaphor, the "light of reason," which seems to have made its home in every intellectual tradition of the human race. In fact, one might well wonder whether this image of the light of reason really is a metaphor at all, a mere illustrative expression. Obviously the expression "light of reason" does not refer to an actual, substantial literal entity with its own content by which man can orient himself. Rather, through this light something else becomes visible, something different from itself, different, that is, from reason as well as from knowledge. This "something else," now visible under the light of reason, is what enables someone to get oriented. Whoever tries to cut a path through the primeval forest will indeed sometimes

43

say he is getting oriented by the light (of the sun during the day, or of the moon and stars at night); but in reality he orients himself by certain landmarks (trees, uneven points in the terrain, roadblocks, etc.) that come into his view *through* the light (and obviously only through the light).

The converse holds as well: that which goes against the light of reason, that which is contrary to reason, in fact contradicts the reality that is recognizable in this light. Reason is the window or mirror through which and in which the objective Logos of things becomes manifest to us. And so it basically amounts to the same thing whether one says: "All laws and customs can be attributed to one thing – the truth"; or says instead: "In every action and transaction, it all depends on the objects being rightly viewed and treated according to their nature."

Both statements, by the way, come from one and the same author, Goethe.[22] As we have seen, this agrees exactly with Thomas Aquinas.[23] Indeed such far-ranging agreement on this point is but the reflection of the entire wisdom tradition of the West.

To be sure, as we have said, only reason (the *lumen rationis*) enables the reality of things to come into view for us. Precisely because the good is that which is commensurate with reality and evil that which works against reality, we cannot escape reason or dispense with it. Reason is not some neutral or passive medium; it is the living power that opens up for us the reality of the world and of existence. Precisely *in* this act of shining its light, reason serves as our Ariadne's thread. It is the norm which nothing else can replace and which remains ever there and unavoidably present, so much so that it even obligates us when it deceives itself (and us)!

The truth of all of these rather elaborate points will

emerge all the more clearly, indeed in a single stroke, as soon as we use another term, the word "conscience," to replace reason or *ratio*, which tends to denote more our specifically cognitive faculty, although clearly both terms are intimately linked. For conscience means nothing other than the power we have by virtue of our own innate reason to render and formulate judgment on what we should do here and now. Sin is an act against reason, which thus means: a violation against one's own conscience, against our "better" knowledge, against the best knowledge of which we are capable.

And even if this judgment of conscience, objectively considered, is in fact *not* the best, even then it still obligates us for as long as there is no other higher authority [*Instanz*] to speak against it. Even if I am determined to direct all my decisions expressly according to the will of God, it is still *my* knowledge and the judgment of *my* conscience in which alone the will of God comes into view for me. And "if reason erroneously (*errans*) says something is God's command, then the demand of reason can no more be disregarded than can God's command." "Every act of the will is simply and always wrong insofar as it does not agree with reason – whether this be in error or not."[25]

Perhaps after the deracinated rationalism of the Enlightenment has brought discredit on *ratio*, we might not feel all that comfortable with this talk of "reason" and being "in conformity with reason." Christians above all have become suspicious of reason, by no means without justification. Nonetheless, one should try to get to know a little more closely what the Great Tradition means by "reason" and what it excludes. First of all, what tradition wants to say about reason does not represent a kind of spiritualizing of reason. Reason neither denigrates the senses nor denies the impenetrable darkness of nature, which we will never, even in principle, be able to master, the depths of which constitute the ground, literally the fundament, of all created beings, very much including the creaturely spirit. Secondly, reason here does not mean the "autonomous," "sovereign," self-realizing consciousness as the vast "System philosophies" of the German Idealists would have it. In the pre-Enlightenment wisdom tradition, reason means receptivity for reality. Finally, reason is not inherently limited to a thinking confined to the realm of the naturally knowable. To be sure, it often depends on the context of the argument whether *ratio* is seen as the partner of faith or its presupposition; but just as often it simply means the ability to grasp the truth, known *or* believed.

Of course, reason can only possess this power to obligate a person if, in the act of knowledge itself, somehow a kind of participation in the divine Logos is taking place and if the interior word-character of things by which we are cognitively oriented to them simultaneously points to the creative aboriginal Word [*Ur-Wort*] of God himself.

One might reply that this is precisely the competence of Christian *theology*. I am not so sure. For example, do not people, whoever they are, bring to a concrete human situation, especially after testing and discerning the matter exactly, a definite decision, calling it either "just" or "unjust"?[26] In other words, by using these word do they not thereby appeal to a final, superhuman court of appeal? Does not such a judgment, rendered with all seriousness, possess an independent obligation on the human subject both by virtue of *what* is being seen in the situation as well as by virtue of the *act* of cognition itself? And does this binding obligation not obligate the knower unconditionally, from within its own source of validity?

III: Contra Naturam, Contra Rationem

Clearly one does not need to be a Christian to be able to see this. Ultimately it was Aristotle who called the superhuman dignity of human reason by name, which he did, not surprisingly, in the context of his ethics: "Reason," he says in the *Nicomachean Ethics*, "is the divine in man."[27]

IV
Contra Deum

Whoever says moral failure is a kind of disorder – and one that brings further disorder in its wake – is no doubt saying something important. As we have seen, moral failure is also something contrary to nature, hindering the realization of what man is meant to be in his life-project of being and becoming human. Finally, moral failure is an *act* (of commission or omission) against the dictates of reason; it goes contrary to better knowledge and thus against one's con-*science*. Moral lapse embodies all of these features, and yet these traits do not really touch on the *essence* of moral failure.

True, all these features of moral failure belong to its subject matter; nothing we have said so far need be withdrawn as, so to speak "missing the mark." But what is decisive and distinctive about sin has as yet gone unmentioned: namely, that it is finally an act directed against God. All the names applied to sin so far are provisional and do not touch on its essence. They can be used without harm as long as one does not understand them as definitive or completely adequate. But as soon as they terminate the analysis, they will not only seem inessential and adventitious but, worse, downright erroneous.

To be sure, the true character of sin might well have emerged in the analysis given so far, at least dimly; and perhaps the reader will have already divined this. Provided the terms "order" and "contrary to order" are energetically tracked down in all their implications, the true nature of sin in its ultimate reality would then emerge easily enough. In other words, we would soon be unable to ignore the fact that sin should be considered a disturbance in man's relationship to his final goal. No longer would we be able to gainsay the conclusion that sin, ultimately, is an *inordinatio quae excludit ordinem finis ultimi*,[1] that is, a reality that in some sense affects our relationship with God.

But this conclusion emerges most clearly and directly if we simply think through in a more radical way sin's reality as something "contrary to nature." Ironically, one cannot help but draw a certain comfort from noticing how Sartre's "existentialism" approaches just this kind of sharper radicality, which claims that there simply is no such thing as human nature, since no personal being preceded the evolution of man; no prior being designed him or intended him to be something definite.[2] On its own terms and inside Sartre's presupposed worldview, the assertion is unimpeachable. It clearly expresses the fundamentals of godless existence far more clearly than a conventional, soothing philosophy that contents itself with holding back from pursuing conclusions to their last consequence. But however unimpeachable on its own terms, the statement is also deeply ironic, for it inadvertently makes clear how an action "contrary to nature" must be, in the final analysis, an infringement against the creative Designer: "The order of nature comes from God himself, wherefore a person does an injustice to God in the act of violating nature: *fit iniuria ipsi Deo, ordinatori naturae*."[3]

If it belongs to the essence of human reason that the reality of the world as well as of ourselves becomes present and palpable to us only in its light and in no other way; and if, moreover, our reason is not a light that *we* ignite on our own but is *communicated* to us, is a participation in that aboriginal light that, as Plato said of the sun,[4] both makes things visible and makes our eyes to see; – then that means, as Aristotle had long ago concluded,[5] that the most decisive characteristic that distinguishes being "in accord with reason" from being "contrary to reason" always depends on whether or not one is directing oneself toward or away from objective reality as well as toward or away from the creative Logos that manifests itself to us in our own power of cognition.

I have cited the names of pre-Christian philosophers here, not without a bit of sly cunning (as does, by the way, Thomas Aquinas too in the same context). For these pagans of antiquity might provide us with the answer to a question that has perhaps already struck the reader as unavoidable. The question, so I imagine the reader formulating it, goes as follows: Why are you lavishing so much attention on the concept of sin being "contrary to order," "against nature," "contrary to reason," when you have just been telling us that these terms are only provisional descriptions of sin that do not touch on its essence? Why not just come right out and label sin with its true and essential name and discuss it on that basis?

Before I try to answer that question, let me first recall a line from Søren Kierkegaard: "Neither the pagan nor the natural man knows what sin is."[6]

This statement finds its relevance at this juncture of the argument not because it represents Kierkegaard's personal view, rooted in his own idiosyncratic theology. Not at all. In fact, it expresses the almost universal opinion among those educated in humane letters [*geistesgeschichtliche Literatur*], although some writers will obviously greet the assertion as a matter to celebrate while others will make their observation in tones of regret. For example, Erwin Rohde says that the ancient Greeks (at least "in their good centuries"!) were "unreceptive" to the "infectious disease of self-consciousness,"[7] and Friedrich Nietzsche praises "Greek antiquity" as "a world without the feeling of sin."[8] Under that interpretation, the pagan's alleged ignorance of the true character of human guilt almost seems like the very definition of happiness in Paradise.

But the same melody can be played on a different instrument at a different tempo, and not just in Kierkegaard. As early as St. Bonaventure's *Commentary on the Sentences* we learn that the Greek philosophers had not known "sin [as] an injury to the divine majesty."[9] And in Kittel's *Theological Dictionary of the New Testament* one reads that "classical Greek civilization" does not know sin "in the sense of hostility toward God."[10]

Yet despite what seems the near universality of this opinion, it is scarcely conceivable how such a thesis can be maintained. Prescinding from all the evidence from other civilizations to be adduced below, we should know how false this thesis is by simply recalling the limpidly told story recounted in Plato's *Symposium* – expressly attributed to Homer but doubtless going back even further – of how the beginnings of human history witnessed an original sin on account of which all subsequent generations inherited a condign punishment. This ancient story was handed down with such absolute clarity and explained the wrath of the gods so unambiguously that Plato claims that the very narration of the story provoked men in their "great thoughts" to "open up a path to heaven to attack the gods."[11]

THE CONCEPT OF SIN

But the same outlook prevails in the non-Western tradition as well. Whether one consults Lao-tzu or Confucius, the Upanishads or the hymns of the ancient Egyptians, the same answer comes back: moral guilt disturbs the way to heaven, it provokes the wrath of the gods, and sets in motion a divinely sent punishment. All of this must surely mean that the true name of moral failure has not remained unknown in various periods of history or been kept hidden from far-distant regions of the world that could have had no contact with each other. And if a monograph in the history of religions[12] summarizes the situation of sin by characterizing it as a "catastrophe" [*Unheil*], what else does human language mean by this word than the loss of that existential attunement that we call "salvation" [*Heil*] and "being whole" [*Heilsein*]?[13] What greater catastrophe could there be than sin's destruction of our final concordance with the divine ground of being without which we know ourselves to be lost along with all that is best in us?

After these intermediate remarks the question we have already formulated can be taken up again. But I hope the remarks made so far, however preliminary or intermediate, have made it at least slightly more fathomable why we have spent so much time, in such detail, on non-essential names for moral failure, and why we have not at the same time mentioned sin's real name. Our intent was to make clear that sin's essential character (acting against God) does not get attached to the guilty person from "the outside," as it were, that is, from a purely theological perspective. On the contrary, an infringement against God is already truly implied and entailed *in* those three characteristics of sin, traits that for mediocre thought are obviously at first the more plausible candidates for describing the essence of sin.

The essential nature of sin is precisely *not* something "totally other," something "completely new," something "utterly different" from what we have discovered about sin in the non-theological phenomenology provided so far. These supposedly non-essential names have a direct bearing on our theme. In short: the thesis that the "natural man" knows nothing of sin proves itself to be – even prescinding from the fact that it can easily be refuted by the data of history – so improbable that no one should have held such a view from the very outset.

Of course the subject matter gets still more complicated when we realize that moral failings [*sittliche Fehlleistung*] ineluctably seem to include the inclination to ignore their own true name.[14] The guilty person wants to protect himself, and so he proves reluctant to call his deed a violation against God (and ultimately against God alone). The last thing the sinner wants is to describe his sin by its true name. Only in moments of true conversion does one say: *Tibi soli peccavi* (Psalm 51:6 – "against you alone have I sinned").

At this point we catch a glimpse of a difficulty: how can sin be recognized as sin at all in the concrete case? This experience is familiar to everyone, but perhaps Goethe has formulated it best when he said that we cannot "see a failing [*Fehler*] for what it is until we are free of it."[15] But this "Everyman-experience" attains an even higher level of truth than one might at first suspect. Simone Weil has made the remarkable observation: "We experience good only by doing it. . . . When we do evil we do not know it – because evil flies from the light."[16]

Perhaps the reader is ready to accept this notion with spontaneous agreement. Nonetheless, the question – perhaps rooted in a shallower region of experience but nonetheless rooted in experience for all that – must still be answered: does man usually think of God in his moral lapses? And if he doesn't, how can we call moral failure by its right name: a action directed against God? Further, *how* should we concretely imagine sin as being *contra Deum*?

As we know, tradition answers with several concepts and images: sin is an insult to God, an act of disobedience to his laws, a turning away from Him, contempt for His being. But do not all these imaginative terms justifiably stand, without exception, under the suspicion of being projections derived from human standards? Are they not all too "anthropomorphic"? Can God really be violated, "nicked" [*angetan*] by man's willing or doing? How is God supposed to be "insulted" by man's "contempt" – indeed, how can God even be *reached*?

Needless to say, no theologian has ever maintained such a thing! Certainly not Thomas Aquinas: "Viewed in strict terms, the action of man can neither provide anything for God nor take anything way from God."[17] He even goes so far as to say that when man expressly places himself against the will of God, not even this act of rebellion, strictly speaking, counts as an event that happens against the will of God: "God's intention cannot be frustrated [*non frustratur*], either in those who sin or in those who attain salvation."[18] This statement is scarcely a notion we can plumb, but again recalls the distinction between "problem" and "mystery."

However, we are not discussing here what moral failure, insofar as it is an *actus contra Deum*, means for God but what it means for man, for his inner existence. And even here the great Western tradition of theology makes decisively clear that "strictly speaking, no one can do God honor or dishonor; nonetheless, this is precisely what we do, insofar as it depends on us, when we surrender our will to God or refuse to do so."[19]

But that still leaves us with our question unanswered: how can sin be *contra Deum* if the sinner is rarely thinking of God, even in rebellion, when he is sinning? Looked at purely empirically, it seems that in the average case only the shadow of a thought of God can be ascertained. In ordinary sins, a person would normally be thinking only of his own advantage, would be worried about making sure his influence and power is felt, would be looking out for *his* pleasure. But he would hardly be thinking of God at the moment, not even so much as would be sufficient for the simple intention to turn away from Him.

V
Pride and Desire

"The essence of guilt consists in voluntarily turning away from God."[1] Under all its numerous modifications, this statement represents the claim of the Great Tradition, unerringly maintained throughout history. In its original Latin the statement uses the term [*aversio*], translated here as "turning away from." But however translated, as a noun ("aversion") or as a gerund ("turning away from"), it is the only term that gets to the core of the issue. It alone definitively specifies what happens in the innermost part of man when he, in the strict sense of the word, "sins."

Straight off, then, we have to ask ourselves once more the question whether it really is part of the essence of sin's character to be an act contrary to God. But before we come at this topic from the empirical side, we first have to ask a more formal question: what is the inner structure of this act of "voluntarily turning away," of this *aversio*, that has here been ascribed to sin? Do moral lapses really have the property, if one analyzes the phenomenon psychologically, of turning away? Does one really ever "turn *away*" from something? Is it not really the case that a person always aims *for* something? Does it not usually happen in the normal course of things that man, insofar as he does something that he should not do, actually wants to *have* some thing? The thief takes something for himself that belongs to someone else. The undisciplined man wants prestige, revenge, intoxicating pleasure. People lie for their own advantage or because they want to be admired.

Where in all this is there even the least trace of deliberately turning away? On the contrary, does not human guilt primarily take on the form of turning *toward* something, of being a kind of *conversio* rather than an *aversio*?

Certainly it does, as the ancients all recognized; so obvious is that reality that it would be inconceivable had they not admitted this. They were well aware of the fact that in man's sin both features are ineluctably linked *de facto*, the act of turning-toward and turning-away.[2] Thomas says so explicitly: "Every sin consists in the longing for a passing good."[3] But at the same time he will insist that a human action does not truly become a *guilty* deed insofar as, and to the extent that, it is a turning toward something. Yes, in every sin there lurks the desire to have and to enjoy, which in fact is why sin can never become definitively bad, a pure evil; this element in every sin of turning toward something is not what makes it to be sin in the strict sense. Formally considered, the concept of sin is instantiated only in the act of turning away.[4]

Why does Thomas Aquinas so emphatically insist that the character of guilt consists in turning away? Because he is precisely the one theologian in the whole tradition of Christian theology who has, in my opinion, more consistently fused this view of sin to his constantly maintained thesis of the creatureliness of man and world. For Thomas there is absolutely nothing in the world that has not been willed, affirmed, creatively loved by the *Creator*; thus there is nothing, precisely as an existing thing [*also seinhaft*], that is not good, and this for no other reason than because it "is."

As a consequence we can never *affirm* something as real in such a way that a human act, or even man himself, would cause it to become "evil." Because the reality of the world is good, because all of its possible intentional objects [*Gegenstände der Zuwendung*] are good too, and because intentionality [*Zuwendung*] itself means that we are always turned toward that good world, for this reason no human deed can ever take on the character of being definitively evil. There is no such thing as definitive evil, guilt, or sin.

That being said, the worldview that ascribes "sinfulness" to "matter" has not exactly gone out of fashion. Manicheeism is no heresy limited to specific centuries or regions of the world. Like all great errors, it accompanies the historical career of the human race as a constant temptation and danger, but especially for Christendom. For Manicheeism, the question of sin's essence is easy to answer: it consists in turning toward the sensible and material, which is evil in and of itself and which thus also "stains" man. But for anyone who is convinced, not only with Thomas but also with the whole New Testament, that "every creature of God is good" (1 Timothy 4:4), such an answer must be rejected out of hand.

The essential goodness of the world, however, is only one side of the coin. The other side of the coin tells us that the ontological goodness of the creature does not just apply solely to the "objective" world of things, of "goods," as we say, encountering us. It also applies no less to ourselves, and that means to our activity as well. But that means that we must ascribe essential good to *every* act of will in the innermost cell of our freedom. In other words, this statement must also hold true for the sinful deed. Oh, the immensity of the thought!

Nor will Thomas shy from this conclusion, for he is

consistent enough in his logic to say: "Evil deeds are good and from God, insofar as we are speaking about what pertains to being."[5] Consequently, not only is there nothing ontologically evil in objective reality to which man could ever direct his intention, but the power of willing is itself of such a kind that, formally speaking, it cannot possibly will evil in the form of positive turning-toward.[6] "Evil is never striven for in the manner of turning toward something, but only by turning away from something. Thus one says something is 'good' by virtue of its participation in the good, but something is 'evil' only by virtue of its distance from the good"[7]– notice how Thomas does not say for example: "by virtue of its participation in evil"!

Therefore, whoever contemplates human actions (including of course one's own deeds) and concentrates solely on the aspect of intentionality, of wanting something "out there," and keeps strictly in view the affirmation behind every action (which certainly is to be found in every sin: as Thomas has already admitted, sin *is* "the longing for a passing good"),[8] whoever sees and considers this side of things, cannot – and this surely by now we should expect! – grasp what is essential to sin. From that perspective, we simply do not see the evil of sin *sensu stricto*. This is why so many people do not regard "sin" as all that damaging, why it starts to take on that mildly facetious connotation we noticed in the opening pages of this essay. Such views are also what lurk behind such common rejoinders as the following: "What is 'sin' when you get right down to it? People just want to keep living and to enjoy life! Why shouldn't they be allowed to get a little fun out of life anyway?"

The clear implication of the above reflections is that no act of turning the will *toward* any of the goods of the world can in fact, strictly considered, be sin unless at the same time this turning-toward is preceded by a turning-away, that is, by deliberately turning away from God.

Of course this juxtaposition of turning-toward and turning-away is not to be thought of in such a way as if in the concrete sinful deed the sinner commits two separate and independent acts of which the one is a turning away from God, making that act thereby the actual evil of the sin, while the other act, the turning toward a creaturely good, is something that can remain good despite the sin. No, the connection between *aversio* and *conversio* is no accidental juxtaposition but an interweaving of both strands into *one* guilty action.[9] For in sin even the act of turning-toward is a distorted act, not of course in and of itself (by virtue of its identity as a turning-toward), but rather because this turning-toward is *meant* to be a deliberate turning away from God.

At this point the question crops up again whether I really have to drag God into the issue to be able to say: look, here is someone sinning, look at this outrage! Take, for example, an extreme case: not just someone who loses mastery over himself (or his automobile) and only ends up hurting himself. But what about the case of the man whose lack of self-control brings his entire family into calamity? Why can't we call that, as the expression goes, "a crying shame" on its own purely "inner-worldly" terms? Do we really have to drag theology into it just so we can condemn this behavior? In other words, isn't there a way of turning toward "creaturely goods" that is inherently disordered, bad, evil, "sin" in the strict sense?

Let's assume then – at least for the moment – the possibility that such an undisciplined "turning-to" has always contained, at least implicitly, the denial of an absolute norm, a norm which it deliberately "turns away from." And let us further assume that sometimes there occurs a disordered "turning-to" creaturely goods that, however disordered in itself, does *not* entail a denial of the Creator. By the way, at this point I am on the verge of inadvertently quoting St. Thomas word for word: "In the case where there is a disordered turning toward a passing good without a turning away from God, then in that case there would be no mortal sin,"[10] although, as was said, the assumption remains in force that such a turning-toward would not be "in order," *quamvis esset inordinata.*[11]

We now meet for the first time the term *peccatum mortale*: "mortal sin" [*Todsünde*], or to use a more literal and less shopworn translation, "deadly sin" [*tödliche Sünde*]. What does this term mean? Before we attempt an answer, we should bear in mind two other concrete names that the tradition uses for naming those two aspects of moral failure: *cupiditas* and *superbia* [desire and pride]: "The name *cupiditas* characterizes sin under the viewpoint of turning toward a passing good; the name *superbia* characterizes sin under the viewpoint of turning from God."[12]

In other words, in every sin both elements, *cupiditas* as well as *superbia*, are both interwoven and interlinked. While the German word for pride *Hoch-mut* [literally, "haughty or elevated mood"] captures fairly well what the Latin means by *super-bia*, it is considerably more difficult to capture in German precisely what is meant by the Latin *cupiditas*.[13] Leaving aside difficulties of translation, what the word refers to is the *already corrupt* desire to have and to enjoy. Such desire has been corrupted because of pride, not the reverse. In other words, only pride – which is a word we use to describe an attitude that intends to turn away from God – makes sin in the first place into the definitive wrong that it is.

Consequently, the less the concrete deed contains the element of "pride" and the more *cupiditas* it has, the less the guiltiness of the action. But the more spiritual a human being is, that is, the more he has rendered himself immune to the seductions and charms of the sensible world by living a life of self-abnegation and disciplining his will, the more he can now commit *the* offense, the sin of unadulterated hybris and blatant pride. Only if all the powers of my being obey me does the question suddenly occur to me: whom do I myself now obey?

This leaves us with an unsettling conclusion: only a purely spiritual being could become guilty in this extreme sense. Of course the philosopher, *qua* philosopher, has no competence to speak of angels and their sin. Nonetheless, we can learn something of philosophical import about the essence of human guilt when theology tells us that the first sin of the angels could only have been the sin of pride.[14]

This teaching of theology bears an important implication when we take up the issue of man's first sin: must not pride be the *principium* of all sin, the primary element, meaning not so much the first in a temporal sense but more importantly the innermost wellspring of sin? But that would mean that every concrete guilt is "fundamentally" pride (taking "fundamentally" quite literally) and that only an act "based on this fundament" is really sin.

No wonder most people have trouble bringing sin into view *as* sin. For one thing, no one disputes how nearly impossible it is to spot the element of *superbia* lurking in all forms of human guilt, especially our own. We blithely assume that our excuses are valid. If in a certain situation we don't tell the truth or if we have betrayed the trust of someone close to us, we think nothing of saying, "Well, it wasn't really half so bad as all that." Let's not fool ourselves: *Qui s'excuse s'accuse.*

But: how does this undoubtedly shameful failure to own up to our guilt imply even so much as a trace of pride? We could no more notice pride in such pretexts (at least at first glance) than we were able to see how we turned from God *in* telling that lie. That both elements cohere together and can be almost one and the same might eventually dawn on us. But how could we have made ourselves guilty of both?

I will try to answer this "disputed question" as follows: Naturally it is impossible to want to turn from God formally and expressly. We cannot keep our attention fixed on such a goal. But still, would it really be beyond human possibility to want to turn from God under some other kind of pretext – using the camouflage term "freedom," for example? Can we really claim that such a mask is completely opaque to our real motives? This at any rate is what the great theological masters ask us to consider. According to Thomas Aquinas, turning from God can become itself the goal "insofar as it is sought under the image of freedom, *sub specie libertatis,* according to the word of Jeremiah: 'From the outset you have smashed the yoke and torn the bonds and said: *non serviam* – I shall *not* serve' [Jeremiah 2:20]."[15] A similar notion holds that concupiscence – our will to possess, whether that be directed to pleasure, honor, ownership, or power – is ultimately rooted in nothing other than in an overweening, disordered *self-love.*[16]

But we still have not proved our case. We have yet to establish how unlimited self-love with its demand for limitless freedom necessarily implies an attack on God. To find this plausible, let alone convincing, we must investigate more deeply the implications of man's creatureliness. In other words, there must be something in man to make him "realize" his own situation; in the midst of the reality in which he finds himself, together with all its consequences, he *chooses*.

But once this insight dawns on him, there can be only two possible answers, at least for a radical, truly "existential" philosophy that does not want to shrink from anything. As Jean-Paul Sartre realized, we are faced with either a clear Yes or a clear No. All intermediate positions eventually prove to be compromises. What is specific to man's creatureliness lies in the fact that he, unlike a crystal, a tree or an animal, can say "I myself." As soon as he does this, that is, in the very moment when he recognizes that his status as a rational animal is unique (on the one hand, he is a creature; on the other, he can either accept or reject this fact), at just that moment he stands before the alternative: he can either choose himself or God.

But this way of putting things still involves us in an impermissible oversimplification. The true alternative rather looks like this: *either* self-realization as surrender to God by recognizing one's own creatureliness; *or* "absolute" self-love by trying to realize oneself by denying or ignoring one's creatureliness. This is *the* fundamental decision *in* every concrete decision, preceding them all. This decision for "absolute" self-love is *the* original sin [*Ur-Sünde*], both in the sense that it was the first ever committed and has also become the very wellspring and fountainhead of all concrete guilt.[17]

In his wonderful book *The Problem of Pain*,[18] C. S. Lewis has tried to visualize man's first sin in paradise. Originally, he says, man's surrender of himself to God required no inner struggle; rather devotion to God was something like "the delicious overcoming of an infinitesimal self-adherence which delighted to be overcome – of which we see a dim analogy in the rapturous mutual self-surrenders of lovers even now."[19] But then at some point humans demanded to have something "of their own." No doubt they would gladly pay God a reasonable tribute for this privilege of ownership in the form of, say, time, attention and love. But in the final analysis it would still be *their* property and not God's. They wanted "to own their own souls."

But that means to live a lie. Our souls are not our own. The first humans wanted a vantage-point, a private corner of their own, in the universe from which they could say to God: "'This is our business and not yours.' But there is no such corner."[20]

Whoever meditates on Lewis's imaginative reconstruction will no doubt be struck by the connection he draws between self-love and rebellion against God. Underneath the mask of self-love, underneath the demand for freedom, there can lurk in truth a self-glorifying and self-asserting resistance against God. *Superbia* and *aversio voluntatis a Deo* really do imply each other. This is sin in the strict sense; here we see sin in its essence, which the whole European intellectual tradition, both pagan and Christian, unites in calling "deadly sin."

VI
Mortal and Venial Sin

I presume the reader was taken aback to read just now that
it is actually the "European intellectual tradition" as a
whole and not just the *Christian* dogmatic tradition that
draws a distinction between deadly sin and its less severe
counterpart. But the distinction appears as early as Plato
(in his interpretation of eschatological myths), and the distinction he draws differs hardly at all from that being made
here. Socrates distinguishes men who have committed
crimes that can be "cured" from those whose crimes cannot
be healed, crimes which render their perpetrators "incurable" as well.[1] Ancient Rome, too, knows of a distinction
between misdeeds that can be "reconciled" and those that
cannot, especially when the discussion centers on cultic
matters.[2]

The question how one can distinguish between these
two kinds of offenses will be taken up shortly, along with
the reasons for the incurability of some sins. But surely it
cannot be mere coincidence that a man like Thomas
Aquinas juxtaposes "mortal" and "venial" sins using
almost the same words as Plato does – a conceptual pairing
that, as everyone knows, has become almost unrecogniz-
able in contemporary society, for it is a distinction that has
now been almost completely obscured by a cloud of misin-
terpretation and sneering. Thomas says the distinction cen-

ters on the contrast of *reparabile-irreparabile* (reparable-irreparable),[3] in other words, curable-incurable. This same vocabulary can be found in the ancient Greeks, who likewise used the word "venial," "forgivable" (*syngnomonikon*). Aristotle speaks of forgivable offenses, ones that have been committed out of ignorance, and distinguishes them from unforgivable sins.[4] Needless to say, he gives not the slightest hint about which authority can vouchsafe or withhold this forgiveness. But he still maintains quite clearly that there *are* offenses of such a kind that deserve forgiveness and others that do not.

So how does the great tradition of Christian theology distinguish between *peccata mortalia* and *peccata venialia*, that is, between "mortal" and "venial" sins? People usually take it for granted that the distinction is basically a matter of "pigeonholing," as if sins had a taxonomy, the way a genus ramifies into various species. Most people assume that just as a genus like "tree" covers different species of trees (beech, birch, oak), so too the word "sin" covers venial and mortal sins equally: in the same way that a beech tree is no more or less a "tree" than a birch or an oak, so specific sins are univocally sins, whether they be mortal or venial.

Now this opinion, however obvious it might seem, Thomas Aquinas flatly declares to be false: "The classification of sins into mortal and venial is not the classification of a genus into species that equally partake of the genus concept," he says.[5] In other words, "mortal" sin is not sin in the same sense as "venial" sin! Well then, what is the difference? "Mortal and venial sins are distinguished within the genus 'sin' in the same way the perfect form is distinguished from the imperfect."[6] "Venial" sin is thus in no way sin in the complete, unabbreviated sense; the *perfecta ratio peccati*, the unmitigated, completely radical concept of "sin" is realized only in "mortal" sin.[7] Nothing more obscures the traditional doctrine of sin than the failure to see this point.

At this point the question naturally arises whether a Christian can speak in the same sense as Plato and Aristotle do of "incurable," "unforgivable" failures. Is the Christian ever permitted to entertain the notion of an unforgivable human guilt? To people living in pre-Christian times – or more exactly, to those living outside the biblical tradition – an answer to the question was never forthcoming. Even the wisdom of the great philosophers fails here, as they necessarily had to stand before this mystery dumb and helpless. Thomas is convinced otherwise and explicitly says so: every human sin, insofar as it can be called "venial," a *peccatum veniale*, can in fact be granted forgiveness.[8]

Nevertheless he remains committed to calling "mortal" sin "irreparable." What he means of course is that *from within its own essence*, from its inherent power to stand fast by its guilt, a healing is not possible – just as we call a disease "mortal" if it can no longer be overcome from within the resources of the sick person, since the very principle of life has been jeopardized and affected by the fatal disease. There are various analogies that might make the matter clearer. For example, if an arithmetic mistake lurks in the very first line of the calculation, in the "principle," then it will never be discovered in any subsequent calculation, no matter how often performed. It can only be found and corrected, so to speak, "from the outside," meaning, only by comparing the erroneous sum with realities outside the calculation itself, that is, only if we completely leave the internal operations of the calculation. But of course that assumes there is such an outer context. "An error in the conclusion can be corrected only on the basis of the truth of the principles"[9] Whereas a mistake located in the principle itself cannot be corrected on the basis of prior calculations – for the very good reason that by definition there is nothing prior to appeal to.

Another comparison: in a political entity [*Gemeinwesen*] there can be two kinds of disorder that for the superficial observer perhaps seems scarcely distinguishable: the one can be cleansed from within, out of the resources of the polity itself; the other not. If the disorder consists in the fact that the prevailing laws are just but are not being strictly enforced and observed, then it is possible to reestablish order on the basis of the healthy principle of the reigning laws. Naturally that does not mean that injustices committed under a just constitution can be downplayed or dismissed as harmless – no more than "venial" sins are to be taken lightly.

But the situation becomes utterly hopeless when the disorder rests on laws that are in themselves unjust. So long as racial discrimination officially prevailed in Nazi Germany on the basis of the notorious "Nuremberg Laws," or as long as a regime officially understands itself to be a "dictatorship of the proletariat,"[10] then the ensuing injustices can never be cleansed from within. The regime simply cannot draw on its own resources, because the evil lurks not in the "conclusion" but in the "principle."

Since man's guilty failings are essentially a disturbance in the *personal* bond with God, we can perhaps best clarify the distinction between "mortal" and "venial" sin by comparing our relationship to God with human friendship or marriage. The Dutch theologian Piet Schoonenberg has demonstrated this in an especially convincing way in his short treatise, *Man and Sin*.[11] The occasional spats and arguments among friends or between two spouses tend on average not to jeopardize or even substantially affect the deeper bond. Neither of the partners thinks of separating himself from the other; "in principle," everything is in order. But there might be more serious disturbances, a serious breach of trust in the friendship or a total rupture in the marriage bond, as when adultery threatens the relationship in its core. Yet even here, a reconciliation, a restoration of the inner unity, would not necessarily have to be entirely excluded, not "in principle." But matters can also come to such a pass that a rupture becomes unbreachable, and the partners are now quite literally "divorced": each one is closed off from the other, in effect "dead." "The same degrees of estrangement may likewise occur between man and his God."[12] This is what the term "deadly" sin is meant to depict.

The author also adds a remark that unexpectedly illuminates the distinction when he points out that in their language the Dutch speak not of "venial" but of *daily* sins. This expression refers to the less significant [*geringfügigeren*] lapses that occur every day but which leave the bond with God basically undisturbed.[13] Furthermore, he says, there may also be "daily" good-deeds that easily co-exist with a breach that is "in-principle" incurable, small deeds that leave the previous rupture unaffected because they can never bridge the gulf or repair the wound. We have all heard of couples who maintain a practiced courtesy to each other but who are living in a dead marriage. So too with God: we can easily maintain a relationship in which a certain "decency" in trivial matters masks a radical turning-away and denial – "mortal" sin.

Strictly speaking, *we* are not the ones who do something in "venial" sin. At least we are not entirely invested

in such sin; we are not entirely ourselves here. The term
"sins of weakness," often used in this context, captures just
this same point. In venial sin we act out of an impulse that
overtakes us. We are more "swept away" than in full pos-
session of our faculties. One might say that "venial" sin
does not actually happen in the innermost center of our
person. In the situation of "mortal" sin, however, the opposite holds true. In fact this terminology of "mortal" sin did
not strike the classical theologians as pressing the matter
deeply enough; and so they described this sin using a word
that might seem in normal usage rather weak: St. Thomas
says "mortal" sin penetrates to "the eternal" in man, *in suo
eterno*.[14] But this turn of phrase, which crops up again centuries later (1923) in a book title by Max Scheler [*The Eternal
in Man*], does not mean something romantic and vague. On
the contrary, it refers to that innermost sanctuary of the
spirit in whose silence the voice of the Absolute Legislator
can alone be heard and in which alone it can therefore be
accepted or rejected.

This is why we can never know who has and who has
not committed a mortal sin. Because human guilt in the full
and strict sense takes place only in the most secret and
silent cell of the deciding person, *in suo eterno*, for that reason "mortal" sin, *peccatum mortale*, is a process hidden from
nature. Nor does it matter how public the sin be: even if the
sin is a blatantly public violation of lawful order, or a violation against the nature of things or the dignity of man,
even if it goes against reason, perhaps even against a divine
commandment; – none of this bears on the accessibility of
mortal sin to human eyes. It stands in no man's power to
judge whether such violations entail a deliberate turning
away from God Himself – sin therefore in the strict, unabbreviated sense. Maybe not even the sinner himself knows!

Perhaps it remains inaccessible not just to the view of another, but also to the reflective consciousness of the guilty person himself, to his *ratio* (perhaps!), even if scarcely to his "heart." God and his own "heart" know of his guilt.[15]

Naturally that should not mean there are also no "objective" criteria that allow one with reasonable care to distinguish between more and less serious offenses. To filch a few pennies from someone; to violate the trust of one's spouse – these are obviously matters of very different import, just as some decisions taken during the course of a day can be quite trivial and others life-determining.

Nor do we wish to say that sin's essential hiddenness means that behavior indicates nothing about someone's state of soul. As Piet Schoonenberg rightly avers,[16] external action is always a sign for what is taking place in the inner core of man. But then again, a sign is always two different things at the same time: announcement *and* cover, unveiling *and* veiling. When looked at from within, the slaying of a human being in the heat of uncontrollable rage, for example, might not be a conscious decision against God, while the mere filching of a few coins could very well, under certain conditions, be a decision fraught with eternal consequences.

This is why I think it worth considering whether we should not all agree to distinguish in ordinary usage between "serious" versus "mortal" (meaning "deadly") sins. We are all perfectly capable of distinguishing felonies from misdemeanors, and similarly we can all objectively determine with sufficient clarity a serious from a trivial offense. But whether a specific human deed is a "mortal" sin, a deliberate turning away from God – that is something

VI: Mortal and Venial Sin

no one can measure except, as we said, God Himself and, perhaps, one's own heart.

The great teachers of Christendom were of one mind in this regard, and they warned us in words like these: "Now which are the sins that 'lead to death' and which are those that do not? – that is given to no human being to decide. 'For who has insight into sin?' [Psalm 19:12 LXX]"[17]

VII

The Paradox of Sin –
A Freely Chosen Compulsion

But now our earlier question returns with an even greater vengeance: how can we even imagine *deliberately* turning away from God, since that would entail the conscious denial of the ground of meaning of our own existence? From our previous analysis, we know very well that historical man is capable of such sin (and that means nothing more than that *we* are capable of it), even if a third party can never identify such sin in us *in concreto*. But now that we realize, based on the reflections in the previous chapter, that sin affects our relationship with the infinite, the question of *why* we sin has become all the more pressing, more difficult, and, so it would seem, more unanswerable. Even if we completely ignore those dogmas that are unique to the teachings of the faith (for example, that sin destroys participation in the life of God – called "grace" in the language of theology[1]); and even if we ignore what the "heart-knowledge" of the saints and poets tell us about sin (figures who are, to use Plato's term,[2] "divine"), namely that sin is a kind of "vampire" (a favorite term of the French novelist Georges Bernanos) whose appetite for blood is insatiable – even if we completely ignore these realities of dogmatic truth or poetic imagery: the phenomenon of sin is still enigmatic enough.

No one claims it is easy to gaze directly on the sheer incomprehensibility of sin without shielding one's eyes or holding back one's full attention. But only in that effort does one begin to see why human beings from time immemorial have tried, however inadequately, to make sense of the nonsensical, to find "rhyme or reason" in what is all too lacking in either rhyme or reason. We have already heard Socrates's answer to this puzzle: that the original cause of human guilt must be ignorance. But that only rationalizes what cannot be made rational, which is why we countered Socrates's answer with Kierkegaard's question: how can we even *use* the word guilt if guilt is based on ignorance?

Kierkegaard's rejoinder certainly sounds plausible, but no less a figure than Thomas Aquinas will agree with Socrates, and frequently, as shown in this catena of citations: "In a certain sense it is true what Socrates says, namely that no one sins with full knowledge."[3] "No sin in the will happens without a kind of ignorance of the understanding."[4] "Always the one who wants the evil chooses it under another name."[5] "Blinding, *excaecatio*, serves as something like the presupposition of sin."[6] Of course Thomas is as convinced as Kierkegaard that humans must be responsible for their actions, which means they can be held accountable and thus liable to punishment and reward; and so he agrees with the biblical verse: "If you were blind, then you would have no sin" (John 9:41).

Another "explanation" says that God himself is the cause of sin, or if not God, then an evil Ultimate Principle with which God is in eternal struggle – scarcely a possible solution, merely an escape hatch, a cul-de-sac. Yet here too there is a "nevertheless" to consider. Does not even the Holy Book of Christianity hold up to our view the frightening idea that God himself has hardened pharaoh's heart

(Exodus 9:12)? And what do we mean when we pray "lead us not into temptation"?

St. Thomas's own reply to this question is unsettling: "The cause of the removal of grace is not due only to the one who resists grace; it is also God who deigns not to bestow grace by virtue of his judging decree. Seen from this perspective, God is the cause of the blindness of the eye, the deafness of the ear, and the hardness of the heart."[7] Of course, these lines represent only one attempt to answer the paradox of willful blindness. But no one, I suspect, will want to dispense himself from letting such a statement penetrate deeply into his heart. Indeed, let no one go astray in the conviction that these matters can be explained! Where does it stand written that *we* are expected to find the "rhyme or reason" in these paradoxes? And if we did come up with an explanation, how would we ever be able to describe it or put it into words?

In any case, things like judgment, atonement [*Sühne*], retribution, punishment by God can exist in some absolute sense only when sin really is what it claims to be: a lapse caused by one's free will, consciously intended, acting contrary to the true sense of one's own existence against order, against nature, against all reason, and most fundamentally against God himself. Try as he may, this is something man has never been able to forget or deny.

But once more, we are still left with the same question: how can so monstrous an act even be thought possible? The question is especially puzzling if one rejects the refuge of saying that reality and existence are in any event entirely and totally absurd to begin with. How can it be that I see the good and also affirm it, but still do what is evil? Most everyone knows that Paul says exactly this, and even laments it (Romans 7:15), but let us not forget its pagan provenance, for the Roman poet Ovid says nearly the same.[8]

The doctrine of original sin comes into play here, for the notion of inherited guilt and punishment seems to explain the paradox. But as we have already seen, the doctrine actually doesn't help to get us very far. To be sure, worldviews that include some kind of inherited fault are a feature of all the traditions of humanity, not just the Judeo-Christian tradition, as is so often ignorantly supposed. I have already mentioned the mythos recounted in Plato's *Symposium*, but other examples can be cited as well: Virgil calls the faithlessness of the Trojan King Laomedon the root of all later evil;[9] Horace calls Prometheus's theft of fire *the* original guilt[10] and says of the murder of Remus[11] that Rome has been stained by this bloody deed at the moment of its founding.[12]

Obviously such views, in their very frequency, show how habitual it is for man to look back to some early sin committed in aboriginal times as the explanation for all later disharmonies and failures of world history. No wonder that the attempt to delimit and measure out the theme of "sin" can never proceed without mentioning the doctrine of original, inherited sin, as Blaise Pascal so well knew: "Doubtless there is nothing more shocking to our reason than to say that the sin of the first man has rendered guilty those who, being so removed from its source, seem incapable of participating in it. Certainly nothing offends us more rudely than this doctrine, and yet without this mystery, the most incomprehensible of all, we are incomprehensible to ourselves."[13]

What is the philosopher to make of a statement like this? If the philosopher won't admit the insights of the Holy

Tradition whose teachings transcend reason, will he not thus have to surrender before the question of how human guilt is metaphysically possible? Certainly Immanuel Kant capitulated when he said, "The origin of the proclivity toward evil remains impenetrable to us."[14] He knew quite well that the attribution of original evil to a tempting demon instigating the first human sin only postpones the problem without solving it, a point he made in the same *opusculum*: "For where did that spirit get its evil?"[15]

Kant usually expresses himself dryly and abstractly, but on this theme he can suddenly seem much more animated. He certainly tells a vivid story when he recounts this fascinating anecdote: Father Charlevoix reports that after he had instructed his Iroquois catechist about all the evil which the wicked spirit had brought into a world created entirely good at the outset and how he was still constantly trying to thwart the best divine intentions, his pupil asked indignantly: "But why doesn't God just strike the devil dead?" – a question for which the priest candidly admits he could, at the moment, find no answer.[16]

In fact no such answer will ever be forthcoming, no matter how much time one devotes to it. For such an answer would have to solve the ultimate enigma: why did God will to create free beings who, by virtue of this same freedom, can turn from him? Nor must we forget that "created" means almost the exact opposite of "striking dead"! It means: cause something to come into existence! But is not *this* our sought-for answer: sin is possible because men are *free* by nature, that is, because that is the way they were created?

Unfortunately, this notion that we must come up with an "answer" is a delusion. At first hearing, Nicholai Hartmann's own answer sounds quite plausible: "There is no freedom for the good that would not be at the same time freedom for evil."[17] But on further reflection we see how the statement introduces an impermissible simplification into the argument. Were this thesis true, then *God* would not be free (nor, for that matter, would the person who has attained final fulfillment, the saint in heaven – a category that only the believer can be convinced of).

In any case, in its long history the Western tradition has conceived of the problem differently from Mr. Hartmann. Thomas Aquinas speaks only as one of its witnesses when he says that to be able to sin is indeed a consequence,[18] or even a sign of freedom, *quoddam libertatis signum,*[19] but "it does not belong to the essence of the free will to be able to decide for evil."[20] "To will evil is neither freedom nor a part of freedom."[21] In other words, the inability to sin should be looked on as the very signature of a higher freedom – contrary to the usual way of conceiving the issue.

To sum up: the negatives of guilt and sin cannot be explained from the positive quality of freedom. And Aquinas's governing assumption [*Vermutung*] that the possibility of sin is more related to a *defect* of freedom[22] does not seem as alien to the experience of the human heart as one might perhaps think. In the journals of André Gide (from which, by the way, I could easily assemble a respectable tractate on sin and evil and even on the evil "one"), the reader comes across this unexpected statement: "Sin is what one does not freely do."[23] Naturally, that is an exaggerated sentence, but it still contains a necessary corrective.

Yes, I admit: we must not forget that sin still gets its origin and springboard from the human will – however much, strictly speaking, it is not committed *as* an act of freedom.[24]

Nowhere have we disputed that in this discussion. Rather, we are simply conceding that we are still left with our initial nagging question: how is an intentional turning away of the will from the very quintessence of all good – toward which the will is inherently oriented by its very nature – even conceivable? How is it possible that the willing person can abuse his freedom so as to decide against the good?

This unsettling question finds in traditional theological anthropology, at least in Thomas Aquinas, an equally unsettling answer: the abuse of freedom, turning away from God, acting against order, nature, and reason, sin in other words, has its ground of possibility in nothing other than in the fact that man is a creature: "Seen from the point of view of its nature, every spiritual creature has the ability to sin."[25] It is because of his creatureliness that man is capable of sinning.

Thomas completes this thought by drawing out its implications in two directions: The *first* concerns, once more, the purely formal structure of making a false step [*Fehlleistung*]. What alone makes possible the deviation from a behavioral norm? In his answer he speaks concretely, almost graphically: "If the hand of the artisan (for example, a woodcutter) were the standard for the woodcut being made, then the artisan could do anything he wanted and would still, by definition, be making the right cut in the wood. But if the rectitude of the cut depends on another standard of correctness, then the cut can be made rightly or wrongly."[26] Extending his argument, Thomas now speaks of the will instead of the hand: Only *the* will can be the right standard of its own willing and must will what is right necessarily, from within itself, and always. A deviation from the norm would not even be thinkable. And obviously only the absolute, divine will is the right standard of its own act.[27]

The converse of the argument should be clear enough: man's will can – just exactly like the cuts made in the wood by the hand of the woodcutter – be right or wrong, good or bad. And for the same reason: because the person doing the willing is a non-absolute being, that is, a creaturely being.

The *second* implication leads even more immediately into the core of the issue under discussion. It begins with this sentence: "The creature is dark, insofar as it stems from nothing."[28] (A strange sentence, that, for those who know nothing of the element of *philosophia negativa* in the world-view of the last great teacher of a still-undivided Christendom![29]) But what does "stem from nothing" mean, if not "to be created"! And precisely *this* – the fact that descent from nothing is inherent in every creature – is the deepest ground for man's capacity for sin, for his *posse peccare*: such is Thomas's opinion.

In other words, not because the will is free, but rather "because the free will comes from nothing, that is why it is inherent to it not to remain in the good by nature."[30] At the same time, of course, Thomas says that such a "bent toward evil" comes to the will "not by virtue of its origin from God, but because of its origin from nothing."[31]

At this point we can hardly suppress the objection: how in the inner structure [*Bauform*] of the created being can we draw a distinction between "origin from God" and "origin from nothing" in such a way that these two origins are placed over *against* each other? Is it not the *Creator* himself who calls things out of nothing and into existence by creating them? We seem to have reached the furthest border beyond which not only language but also thought itself begins to encounter the impassable.

THE CONCEPT OF SIN

What then of our question? If we look back on the path taken so far, we can say that, in a fundamental sense, the question will always remain unanswered, at least if we mean by "answer" some piece of information through which our questioning can be stilled and soothed. All we can do is admit that we are faced with, so to speak, a *reductio ad mysterium*. We are now at the very threshold of mystery in the strict sense, one that cannot be further illumined. At this point, we either respect and honor it, or deny and reject it.

VIII
The Stain of Sin

By its very nature sin cannot be confined to the time span of the guilty act itself. With the act of sin something comes into existence that remains and lives on. Perhaps there is a "Now," inaccessible to temporal measurement, where decisions of the will take place, where actions flowing from these decisions become sinful or not. If so, this Now cannot gainsay what humanity has never denied: that the evil of sin does not perish with the sinful act. Sin's effects cannot be so easily "dispatched" as that.

I am not simply referring to such obvious cases as sins of the tongue. We all know that a well-aimed slander, perhaps set in motion by a curt remark tossed off in an unguarded moment, lives on long after: people continue to believe it, it gets passed on from mouth to mouth, harming the victim at each turn – and so on. No, examples like these refer to sin's continued effects in objective reality. But sometimes, often by sheer accident, these effects gradually begin to dissipate under the leveling power of time's inexorable elapse, forgotten not only by the "people" but perhaps even by the victim himself.

My focus at this point concerns not so much the effects in the victim of sin as in the soul of the sinner. To return to the case of the slanderer: his guilt does not just wound the feelings and reputation of his victim but warps his own soul like a wound or a stain. Whatever name one wants to call it, the soul is permanently marked by sin. The ancients preferred the word *macula*: a blot, a stain. "Sin should be considered under two aspects: the guilty act and the *macula* derived from it," so Thomas Aquinas.[1] Once again we must stress that this is not a specifically Christian thought. In the mythical story that Plato's Socrates recounts at the end of the *Gorgias*, exactly the same thing is said: when someone lies or fornicates, commits perjury, or perpetrates violence, something sticks to the soul, warping and distorting her. And when the souls depart for the Underworld, the judges of the dead notice these scars as if they were the wounds left over from the lash of the scourge.[2]

Our question, therefore, must be: what kind of being, what ontological status, does this stain have that bears so many names in the tradition? Obviously it is a reality not easily described. Is it even a "reality" at all? "Not in the positive sense," one is informed by Thomas Aquinas: "not in the positive sense does anything remain in the soul after the act of sin: *nihil positive remanet in anima*."[3] Rather, a "deprivation" remains, a *privatio*, the loss of something that should not have been lacking.

It goes without saying that the word *macula* can be misinterpreted as denoting something positive. This was the error of the Manichees, who held that the soul was stained by touching a reality itself impure and evil. Thomas sees the danger of this view and so sharply replies: the soul is not stained by "lower" things; rather the reverse: "the soul stains herself by her own action."[4]

Because stains and dirt have a positive reality of their own, the Manichees might seem to have a point. But we can get a better idea of what ordinary language and the mental habits reflected in daily usage mean by the word "stain" if we contrast it with the image of light and its radiance. In other words, people most often use the word "spot" negatively, not to point out something positive but normally when an article of clothing or a gold or silver object has lost its shine at a particular place.[5] So too with the human soul: the soul can lose her radiance, in this case a radiance that is due not only to the light of natural reason but also to the divine light.

Now it is precisely the *macula* that remains with sin; sin causes a "matting" [*Verdüsterung*], so to speak, of the brightness radiating forth from this twofold light. "But if man returns to the light of reason and to the divine light by virtue of grace, then the stain is washed away."[6]

"If man returns . . ." This allusion to "return" recalls another image by which the lasting effects of sin have also been named: distance from God, the *distantio a Deo*.[7] The *movement* of distancing oneself that takes place in the act of sinning ceases as soon as the sin has been committed, and then it belongs to the past. But the state of *being* distant continues on; for it is the nature of distance to remain what it is as long as one stays put. Distance cannot be overcome if one just stays standing where one is.

If mortal sin really does exclude someone from the kingdom of God,[8] then that means the sinner is now "outside." Obviously this fact of "being outside" remains as an ongoing, continuing *factum*. It could hardly be abolished simply by ceasing to sin. Nor can distance be overcome by suppressing the memory of the guilty act, and still less can it be magically transformed into a new state of being "inside" unless the soul first sets out on a journey whose length is determined by that very distance brought about by sin.

Perhaps it belongs to man's ineradicable powers of self-deception to hold that moral guilt can disappear "by itself," as if sin came with some kind of "statute of limitations" (as when we use the proverbial expression "the grass will grow over it"). Obviously something else must occur, or more exactly, something must *be* done if the soul, to speak with Plato, is to get rid of her scars and warts, if she is to get back her radiance [*Lichtheit*], if her nearness to God and her membership in God's kingdom is to be restored.

This need of the soul to undertake an expiating journey of return introduces a new theme, a theme to be taken up shortly. But we must still consider a few other names and images for that perduring element that continues on after the act of sinning is over. For instance, the tradition speaks of a condition of bondage and imprisonment[9] that the soul has brought upon herself by sinning – a view that seems especially convincing to raw experience. Once more we quote from the journals of André Gide, who knows this experience well: "The Evil One kidnaps us for his cause and puts us in his service. Who dares to speak of liberation here? . . . As if vice were not more tyrannical than duty!"[10]

Sin does more than this, however. Sin not only stains the soul with a lasting blemish as soon as a sin is committed; it not only darkens her light, distances her from God, and sells her into bondage (and also, as theology says, weakens the soul's receptivity for grace, creating a *diminutio aptitudinis ad gratiam*[11]). Most crucially of all, sin effects a still deeper ontological transformation, one that penetrates the very core of the person, branding the soul with a property which the ancients call, using a term that has become completely outmoded today but whose pedigree goes back to classical times – *reatus*.[12]

The word derives from *reus*, guilty, and it means the

condition of being guilty. Sin doesn't just mean: I have *done* something. Sin also means: I henceforth *am* something that I was not previously: I am, because of my deed, guilty. The status of being guilty is what "springs out of" the act of sinning as its inner fruit, its *effectus*. "When one says that sin, as an act, is something that expires but as *reatus* is something that perdures, then this amounts to saying that sin expires in what it is, but perdures in what it effects."[13]

If the word *reatus* serves to denote the ongoing status of being guilty, then it must imply the need for punishment as well. Ordinary language often implies the same thing when it says of a criminal that he is not only "guilty of murder" but also is "guilty of death."[14] So *reatus* – as an inner, lasting fruit of sin – means a twofold personal quality,[15] both of being guilty, of "having" guilt, as well as of deserving punishment, the *obligatio ad poenam*.[16] Father Scheeben has defined this obscure term as a "liability before God based on one's indebtedness."[17]

But whether one speaks of "liability" or of being "worthy of punishment" or even, with the ancient Romans, of the "curse" (of the gods), the intellectual traditions of mankind speak unanimously of a necessary ordering of guilt to expiation, which for the Latins was expressed by the word *reatus*. As the historian Theodor Mommsen has shown,[18] the entire penal code of ancient Rome was based on the idea of *expiatio*; for the Romans this word indicated their belief that the "curse" still polluting the city in the wake of a crime could only be deflected from the community through punishment and expiation.

Of course that still leaves open the question which authority is competent to judge human guilt (taking "guilt" in its strict sense). Who should pass sentence and specify the expiation? This question obviously bears on the neural-gic topic of how the state should legislate its penal code: *quis custodiet custodes?*[19] One might well raise justified doubts, either as a philosopher or psychologist, about whether any human being can incur "pure" guilt. Can any man ever violate the good without an element of weakness coming into play? When is a criminal never swept away, tempted, "determined"?

If, however, there is guilt and sin in the unmitigated sense, then there must necessarily also be expiation and punishment in its wake, at least if these words are to have any meaning. Nor is this (essentially semantic) point at all undermined because we might never be certain of the answer to the question *who* might be the competent author-ity to specify and execute that punishment. Guilt and sin are something that by their nature call for punishment. This view has been so completely taken for granted by the consensus of mankind from time immemorial that we do not need to spend any more time discussing it.

What about hell? The idea of guilt might automatically entail the idea of punishment, but *unending* punishment? Certainly no consensus reigns here, at least nowadays. Previously, however, eternal punishment was commonly considered to be the fitting expiating punishment justified by a mortal sin committed with full intent of the will. Nor again was this just the consensus of the Christian tradition; the eschatological myths recounted by Plato also ascribe to "incurable" crimes a temporally unlimited punishment, *eis aei chronon*[20] (which Schleiermacher literally translated, and vividly, as "for always time").

Naturally theologians will need to interpret traditional dogmatic statements about "eternal damnation" according to their true intentionality. Although this task pertains to the competence of the theologian, a philosophical anthropology will have to take careful cognizance of this *theologoumenon* [crux of theological interpretation], since such a doctrine has so much to say about the inner form of man's moral failings.

So if we feel compelled to discuss the punishment of damnation (or, to speak without euphemism, of "hell") in the next few pages, then we had better first make sure that a purely emotional opposition to the doctrine of hell not block genuine understanding. To this end we make two observations.

First: eternal punishment applies only to "deadly" sin in the strict sense; that is, only when the sinner consistently maintains his sin, consciously turning away from God's will. If we are ever going to recognize an inherent connection between hell and mortal sin, we must first see how every mortal sin entails what one might call an "eternity-intention." To sin "mortally" means: deliberately to apply the most intense valuation and love of which one is capable not to God but to oneself.

To qualify as truly "deadly," this decision against God must go all the way to the roots and shirk from nothing. It must be a decision so radical that its only analogue at the opposite pole would be the decision of a martyr or blood-witness: in both cases it is a matter of life and death. Whoever loves something to the furthest limit wills to have it *forever*.[21] Which means that mortal sin, when realized to its ultimate consequence, likewise "wills eternity."

Recall what we said earlier about man's innermost "eternal" center as the location for deadly sin. Now we see why. The sinner must be willing not only to persevere in sin all the way through this earthy life, but he must also want to persevere in his sin "into eternity," *in aeternum*.[22] It belongs to the nature of this act to intend something definitive and thus to be "irreparable." The definitiveness of punishment only matches the definitiveness of the decision.

Second: when discussing "eternal punishment" one must clearly distinguish the images that are meant to make the essence of the matter visible to the imagination from the essence of the matter itself. But if the essence of damnation is rightly characterized as separation from the infinite Good, which God himself is,[23] then the punishment only consists in not possessing what one has already expressly renounced. "Hell" should not be thought of as a dungeon inside which one has been forcibly locked up against one's will. The bolt on the door that seals off the way into the open air is not located outside, but inside, the person. It is the stiff-necked will of the damned person himself, a will that turns away from God, which has closed the gates of hell in on itself.

Again we must point out that this insight is not specific to the Christian tradition, but belongs to everyone. It is not unknown even to Jean Paul Sartre. In his drama *No Exit* (*Huit clos*), none of the three damned souls leaves the oppressive hotel-room (hell) when the door suddenly springs open, even though all of them had just previously been passionately crying out to be freed. André Gide, whose journals we quote one last time and whose ruthless honesty reach their high point here, calls hell "sinning on and on, against one's better knowledge and without any real desire to do so."[24]

These two modern Frenchmen, each in his own way, confirm the traditional wisdom according to which hell consists in man being taken at his word when he refuses to love. The following citation does not come from one of the Church Fathers, but from Dostoyevsky's novel *The Brothers Karamazov*: "You fathers and teachers, what is hell? I think it is the pain of no longer being able to love."[25]

The simplest and most striking formulation of the meaning of hell, not only in the originality of its diction but also because it so completely agrees with the Great Tradition, can be found in C. S. Lewis's book *The Problem of Pain*, which obviously could not pass over in silence the problem of hell, the most extreme example of pain. Indeed he begins by saying: "There is no doctrine which I would more willingly remove from Christianity than this, if it lay in my power."[26] But then he directs a few questions to the one who protests against this view of "hell":

In the long run the answer to all those who object to the doctrine of hell is itself a question: "What are you asking God to do? To wipe out their past sins and, at all costs, to give them a fresh start, smoothing every difficulty and offering every miraculous help? But He has done so, on Calvary. To forgive them? They will not be forgiven. To leave them alone? Alas, I am afraid that is what He does."[27]

This word "forgive," apparently dropped here so casually by Lewis, summons up a couple of more questions for us to consider. That forgiveness can be vouchsafed only to the one who wants it, or at least is willing to accept it, is perfectly obvious to everyone. If someone were to be forgiven who does not want forgiveness, that would mean declaring him literally incapable of assuming responsibility for himself.

Much more pressing, however, is the other question: how can guilt be purged from the world, how it can be healed and extinguished? Through forgiveness. Obviously healing first presupposes the capacity to be healed and thus the non-fatal nature of the disease. But as we pointed out earlier, does it not belong to the essence of fully intended sin to be a definitive, "irreparable" decision?

Both dimensions are indisputably true. But at least in man's case, whose decisions indeed *can* be definitive but which have not yet *become* so, the intention to make a definitive decision can change. But then if human beings can change their mind, for whom does the concept of absolutely definitive decision apply? Once more we confront the limit-concept of the sin of pure spirit. According to theological tradition, the sin of a pure spirit is by nature incurable, *irremediabile*,[28] because only a purely spiritual being, an angel in other words, is capable of an absolutely definitive decision. That means that only in the case of the pure spirit can there be guilt in the full unmitigated sense of an irrevocable decision against God. Only pure spirit possesses an essence allowing for this kind of irrevocable decision.

We have introduced the theological theme of the sin of the angels at this point not for its own sake (that should go without saying), but rather to draw a perhaps surprising connection between Lucifer's sin and an anthropology that seeks to glorify man's autonomy. For some philosophers hold that, at least in the realm of knowledge and decision-making, man is just as much a pure spirit, just as much a sovereign subject as theology claims for pure spirits. This anthropology does not flinch from drawing the uncanny consequence that man should reject every possible forgiveness of his guilt as something unworthy of him as a human being:

Once one has taken it [guilt] upon oneself, then one cannot let it be removed without negating oneself. The guilty person has a right to bear his own guilt. He must reject any redemption from the outside. Along with giving up the guilt, he would also be giving up the greater moral good, his humanity. . . . Redemption infantilizes man, hands him over to the abandonment of his freedom.[29]

Let us not consider the person of the author, Nicholai Hartmann, whom no one is competent to judge (I trust that goes without saying). Instead, let us take these terrifying sentences just as they stand. If we do so, then we will recognize in them exactly what the Western Christian tradition says is the attitude of the fallen angels and of the souls eternally damned: that the forgiveness of their guilt is impossible since it would be rejected by them as an unreasonable humiliation and imposition, because, in other words, the guilty person wants to stand by his decision made against God.

> . . . *Farewell, happy fields*
> *Where joy for ever dwells: hail horrors, hail*
> *Infernal world, and thou profoundest hell*
> *Receive thy new possessor: one who brings*
> *A mind not to be changed by place or time.*
> *The mind is its own place, and in itself*
> *Can make a heaven of hell, a hell of heaven.*
> *. . . Here we may reign secure, and in my choice*
> *To reign is worth ambition, though in hell:*
> *Better to reign in hell than serve in heaven.*

But if we assume that there could be true healing, purgation, extinction of guilt for human failings, even for "mortal" failure, we are still left with the question how we might imagine it as something like a real possibility. What conditions would have to be fulfilled so that forgiveness, real forgiveness, could take place?

The first presupposition should be familiar to everyone: it is called knowledge, recognition, and abhorrence of one's own guilt. Let us cite once more Simone Weil: "We experience good only by doing it. We experience evil only by refusing to allow ourselves to do it, or if we do it, by repenting of it."[30] Repentance, the express disapproval of one's own sin, is always possible to man, no matter how much he means his guilty act to be irrevocable. Here again we see his great difference from the purely spiritual beings who cannot "rue" their sin. As Thomas puts it: "They cannot dislike their sin."[31]

But what an unsettling thought it is when we consider how close the demonic inability to convert is to man's self-misinterpretation as an autonomous being of pure spirit! Friedrich Nietzsche made himself its evangelist, he proclaimed it as the "gay science." "Better to remain guilty," he says, "than to pay with a coin that bears not our image – so much does it want our sovereignty."[32]

How much could be said of this new evangel! But let us be content with just this observation: contrition means nothing other than exactly this, that we "pay with a coin that bears *our* image." *We* are the ones who say no to *our own* guilty deed.

Again, this insight belongs to the common fund of wisdom of all humanity. Speaking just of the West, Plato's Socrates contradicts in his own person Nietzsche's thesis that the Greeks would have rejected contrition as a "slave affair." And the Far East has its own conviction that contrition is an indispensable existential act of health, summarized with peerless clarity in this incomparable line: "First realize you are sick, then you can move toward health."[33]

If contrition is indispensable for healing the wounds and disease caused by guilt and sin, an equally indispensable condition for inner freedom must also be self-accusation, the admission of one's own guilt, the face-to-face confession before another person. This too seems to be a component of the wisdom tradition throughout the history of the entire human race, very much including the pre-Christian and non-Christian worlds. According to a Hindu rule the neophyte monk is supposed to reveal his failings to the *guru*. Plutarch says of the mysteries of Samothrace that the initiate must confess to the cultic priest the worst faults of his life.[34] In Lydia and Phrygia, steles and stone tablets from pre-Christian times have been found on which confessions of guilt have been inscribed, available for any passer-by to read.[35] Again, Plato's Socrates requires not only that the one who has done an injustice take upon himself without complaint a severe punishment but also – in order to get free of his injustice – that he be his own foremost accuser against himself.[36] If a rhetorician were to do *that*, Socrates tartly observes, he would finally be showing the city a beneficial application of the art of speaking![37]

Christians have recently been heatedly debating the value of "public acts of penance" and "personal confession." Not surprisingly, many claim that such concrete acts of public self-accusation are demeaning to man. But anyone who seeks to analyze the unspoken arguments behind these contemporary debates will soon discover how much people know of its necessity.

Yet because sin not only wounds an objective, neutral

norm but also attacks a personal Someone, neither contrition nor confession – both of which are unilateral acts – can alone suffice for making someone truly free of his guilt. For that purpose the "Other" must also do something from his side – although an indispensable prerequisite for liberation has of course been fulfilled when the sinner, so to speak, "unilaterally" recognizes and disapproves of his guilt. No restoration or redress is possible unless the guilty person call his sin by its true name. But that having been said, the person impaired by the sin must respond as well, or the relationship will never be restored.

On this point, it seems to me, psychotherapeutic theory and praxis propagate influential misunderstandings. Some time ago I was visiting a highly regarded psychotherapist, famous for his elegant and polished writings, at his Frankfurt home. There, on a platform almost as elaborately decorated as the stage of an opera house, I came across Edward von Steinles's well-known painting, *The Great Penitent*, which depicts an ecclesiastical dignitary vested in purple and at his side someone kneeling and whispering his confession of sins.

With ironic admiration and probably an unconcealed surprise, I was contemplating the old-fashioned, ceremonious scene when my host candidly told me, not without a slight hint of smugness, that this scene depicted what his job was like day in and day out. I could not suppress my astonished rhetorical question whether he had the competence to say to his patients: *Ego te absolvo* – "I absolve you from your sins."

With this word from the rite of the sacrament of confession we have come to the border, and perhaps overstepped it, marking off theology from philosophy. In any case, it transcends the competence of the philosopher to speak expressly of sacramental absolution. But whoever reflects on the phenomenon of human failing, keeping his mind open to all its aspects, can expect that the supra-rational dimension of the object will finally emerge into view. If we realize that perfectly consummated human guilt finally means a decision against God, and ultimately against Him alone, then it will suddenly dawn on us that man's sin – despite his contrition and confession of guilt – can really only be extinguished by one act, by one act alone: the gift of forgiveness freely bestowed on us by God him-self.

Notes

I: Usage

1. Paul Valéry, "Über die Tugend," *Europäische Revue*, Vol. 11 (1935).

2. H. H. Hanson, "Schuld en Boeten in het oude Rome," in *Donum Lustrale Catholicae Universitati Noviomagensi oblatum* (Nijmegen 1949).

3. Thomas Mann, *Briefe 1889–1936* (Frankfurt), p. 234.

4. Friedrich von Hügel, *Religion als Ganzheit*, edited by Maria Schlüter-Hermkes (Düsseldorf, 1948), p. 348.

5. Ernst Jünger, *Der Gordische Knoten* (Frankfurt, 1953), p. 118. (Jünger was a German officer in World War I. At the outbreak of World War II in 1939, he rejoined the army at the rank of captain but was dismissed by the Wehrmacht in 1944. After both wars he wrote extensively of his experiences and views. Many of his works, including the work cited here, are introspective broodings in essay form. He is most famous for his 1939 allegorical anti-totalitarian novel *Auf den Marmorklippen* [trans. note].)

6. Nicholai Hartmann, *Ethik*, 3rd edition (Berlin, 1949), p. 818.

7. Martin Heidegger, *Sein und Zeit*, 6th edition (Tübingen, 1949), p. 306.

8. *Ethik*, p. 817.

9. *Summa Theologiae*, III, 46, 2 ad 3.

10. Immanuel Kant, *Die Religion innerhalb der Grenzen der blossen*

Vernunft, ed. Karl Vorländer, 5th edition (Leipzig, 1950), pp. 44–45; translated as *Religion within the Limits of Reason Alone* by Theodore M. Greene and Hoyt H. Hudson (LaSalle, Ill.: The Open Court Publishing Company, 1934), p. 37.

11. Søren Kierkegaard, *Die Krankheit zum Tode*, ed. J. Frieser (Bremen, 1949), p. 89; translated as *Sickness unto Death* by Walter Lowrie (Princeton: Princeton University Press, 1941), p. 162.

12. Hartmann, *Ethik*, p. 811.

13. Ibid., p. 817.

14. Ibid., p. 819.

15. Ibid., p. 819.

16. Friedrich Nietzsche, *Also Sprach Zarathustra*, Part III: "Von der grossen Sehnsucht."

17. *Gedanken über Moral* (1880–1881). *Gesammelte Werke* Musarion-Ausgabe (Munich, 1922), Vol 10, p. 427.

18. *Morgenröte* 3, 202.

19. Hartmann, *Ethik*, p. 820.

20. Ibid., p. 817.

II: Missing the Mark

1. See, for example, Richard C. French, *Synonyma des Neuen Testaments* (Tübingen, 1907), p. 153.

2. Aristotle, *Nicomachean Ethics* 2, 6; 1107a15,

3. Volume I, p. 271. The entry under this word also says, by way of summary: "the usual term for sin does not therefore possess the predominantly religious connotation that is proper to the German word" [or the English word; translator's note].

4. Thomas Aquinas, *De malo* 2, 2.

5. Aquinas, *Compendium theologiae* I, 119, # 235.

6. Aquinas, *De malo* 2, 2. Similarly ST I/II 21, 2: "As the concept *malum* has a wider range of meaning than the concept *peccatum*, so too does the concept *peccatum* have a wider range than the concept *culpa*."

7. Aquinas, *De malo* 2, 2.

8. And of course under this rubric we are only referring to *artistic* failings as such, *peccata artis* (*De malo* 2, 2); whoever has nothing else in mind than random shooting in the air obviously can't be said to be misfiring, at least in the sense of "artistic" failure!

9. Eugen Herrigel, *Zen in der Kunst des Bogenschiessens* (Constance, 1948). Translated as *Zen in the Art of Archery* (New York: Random House).

10. Aquinas, *De malo* 2, 1: "Magis est de ratione peccati, praeterire regulam actionis quam etiam deficere ab actionis fine." (In accordance with Thomas's specialized use of *peccatum* to mean any false step whatever, the author has translated the Latin word with *Fehlleistung*, translated here as false or misdirected step. I have therefore translated Pieper's German and not Thomas's Latin [translator's note]).

11. *Zugespitzt*: I presume the author is making an archery pun here, as this is the first word of the sentence, although perhaps it is unintentional (translator's note).

12. Thomas Aquinas, *De malo* 2, 2: "Rationem culpae non habet peccatum nisi ex eo quod est voluntarium." (Translated in the author's mode, the line might read something like this: "Misfire does not bear the essence of sin unless it is voluntary" [translator's note].)

13. *Summa theologiae* I/II, 21, 2, obj. 2: "Artifex non culpatur ex hoc quod aliquid malum facit." See, as well, *ST* I/II, 21, 2, ad 2.

14. Ibid.

15. Actually this list could be extended to a few moderns, who

try to maintain the old usage, for example, T. S. Eliot and Gottfried Benn.

16. "From a technical point of view it was a sweet and lovely and beautiful job." Transcript of remarks by J. Robert Oppenheimer before the Personnel Security Board, *In the Matter of J. Robert Oppenheimer* (Washington, D.C., 1954), p. 229. (Pieper used the phrase "technically sweet" in its original English [translator's note].)

17. Of course that is only an inexact way of putting it: only man, after all, can be (in the moral sense) good or bad, not a book. Nonetheless, it should be clear what is meant.

18. *Summa theologiae* I/II 21, 2, obj. 2.

19. Ibid, ad 2.

20. Günther Anders, *Endzeit and Zeitende: Gedanken über die atomare Situation* (Munich, 1972), p. 82.

21. Ibid., p. 101.

22. Rudolf Höß, *Kommandant in Auschwitz: Autobiographische Aufzeichnungen* (Stuttgart, 1958), above all pp. 93 ff, 120, 160 ff.

23. Quoted in Hans Lenk, *Philosophie in technologischen Zeitalter* (Stuttgart, 1971), p. 20.

24. Martin Buber, *Bilder von Gut und Böse. Werke*, Vol. I (Munich, Heidelberg, 1962), p. 620.

25. *ST* I/II 72, 1 ad 2; similar to I/II 75, 1 ad 1 (Pieper's brackets [translator's note]).

26. *ST* I/II 21, 1 ad 3.

27. *ST* I 82, 1 ad 3.

28. Malum culpae facit hominem simpliciter malum. *De malo* 1, 5.

29. Aquinas, *De veritate* 25, 5.

30. Ibid.

31. *Sickness Unto Death*, p. 144.

32. Pierre Teilhard de Chardin, *La pensée du Père Teilhard de Chardin, par lui-même.* Vol 10: *Les Études Philosophiques* (Paris, 1955), #4.

33. *Thus Spake Zarathustra,* Part IV, "On the Higher Man," #5.

III: Contra Naturam

1. *Actus inordinatus.* Thomas Aquinas, *ST* I/II 71, 1; *De malo* 2, 9 ad 2; *De veritate* 25, 5.

2. *De malo* 7, 1.

3. *ST* I/II 77, 4.

4. *ST* II/II 125, 2.

5. Ordo non est substantia, sed relatio. *ST* I 116, 2 ad 3.

6. Augustine, *De libero arbitrio*, *PL* (Migne) 32, 1290. (It might seem odd to the reader that Pieper includes Thomas Aquinas in the first Christian millennium, since he lived in the second, but presumably the author is referring to a theological millennium beginning just before Augustine's time [translator's note].)

7. *ST* I/II 78, 3.

8. *ST* II/II 130, 1.

9. The etymology of the Greek term for nature, *physis*, stresses growth since it comes from the Greek verb to grow, *phuo*; while the Latin word for nature, *natura*, stresses birth since it comes from the Latin participle for born, *natus*. The author is here drawing on both realities encompassed by the concept of nature (translator's note).

10. *ST* I/II 109, 2 ad 2.

11. The equally possible translation for *inclinatio naturalis* as a "*natural* inclination" is misleading because it does not express the character of an event of nature. But to say "of nature" brings out the kind of event of nature one sees, for example, when a star falls. (The author is making a distinc-

tion here between *naturhaft* and *natürlich*, one that is unique to him, as these two words seem interchangeable to this translator's ear; in any event the English "natural" connotes both meanings, so I use the slightly paraphrastic expression "of nature" to bring out Pieper's distinction [translator's note].)

12. *ST* II/II 131, 1.

13. Kierkegaard, *Purity of Heart Is to Will One Thing: An Edifying Discourse,* translated by Douglas V. Steere (New York: Harper & Row, 1938).

14. Ibid., p. 22.

15. Roger Garaudy, *From Anathema to Dialogue: A Marxist Challenge to the Christian Churches,* translated by Luke O'Neill (New York: Herder and Herder, 1966).

16. Josef Pieper, "Herkunftlose Zukunft und Hoffnung ohne Grund?" In: *Über die Schwierigkeit, heute zu glauben: Aufsätze und Reden* (Munich, 1974), pp. 179 ff.

17. Aquinas, *De malo* 8, 2.

18. See, for example, *ST* II/II 153, 2; II/II 168, 4.

19. See Thomas Aquinas's commentary on the passage, *In De divinis nominibus* (Turin, 1950) Section 32, # 245 ff.

20. Facit rationem peccati: *ST* II/II 162, 1.

21. Thomas Aquinas, *Commentary on the Sentences of Peter Lombard* 2d. 42, 1, 4 ad 3.

22. From a letter to F. von Müller of 28 March 1819, in: *Maximen und Reflexionen,* edited by Günther Müller (Stuttgart, 1945), # 530. The original reads: "Alle Gesetze und Sittenregeln lassen sich auf eine zurückzuführen: auf die Wahrheit." "Im Tun und Handeln kommt alles darauf an, dass die Objeckte rein aufgefasst und ihrer Natur gemäss behandelt werden."

23. See as well Romano Guardini, "Klassischer Geist," in: *Die Schild-genossen,* Volume 5 (1924).

24. *ST* I/II 19, 5 ad 2.
25. *ST* I/II 19, 5.
26. See Emil Brunner, *Gerechtigkeit* (Zurich, 1943), p. 54.
27. Aristotle, *Nicomachean Ethics* Book 10, 7; 1177b.

IV: Contra Deum

1. *De malo* 15, 2: a disorder that blocks our orderedness to our ultimate end.
2. Jean-Paul Sartre, *L'existentialisme est un humainisme* (Paris, 1946), p. 22.
3. *ST* II/II 154, 12 ad 1.
4. Plato, *Republic* 508 f.
5. Aristotle, *Nicomachean Ethics* 10, 7; 1177b.
6. Kierkegaard, *Sickness Unto Death*, p. 144.
7. Erwin Rohde, *Psyche*, tenth edition (Tübingen, 1925), Vol. I, p. 319.
8. Friedrich Nietzsche, *The Gay Science* 3, 135.
9. Bonaventure, *Commentary on the Sentences of Peter Lombard*, 2d, 38, 1.
10. *Theological Dictionary of the New Testament*, Vol. I, p. 299.
11. Plato, *Symposium*, 190b–c.
12. Gustav Mensching, *Die Idee der Sünde* (Leipzig, 1931), p. 22.
13. This play on words works much better in German than English, but readers will be helped to understand the author's point if they realize that the English words for "whole," "health," and "holy" come from the same Indo-European root as the German word *Heil*, which is the standard theological term in German for salvation, while *heilig* mean "holy" and is the standard prefix title for a saint. *Unheil* is equally generic and means any misalignment of that right functioning denoted by "health" and "whole," and can mean

anything from nausea ("Ich fühle mich unheil") to a cata-strophic disaster like an earthquake (translator's note).

14. Karl Rahner, "Schuld und Vergebung," in: *Anima* 8 (1953), p. 259.

15. Goethe, *Dichtung und Wahrheit* 2, 8: "Wir können einen Fehler nicht eher einsehen, als bis wir ihn los sind." (The word *Fehler* is usually translated as "mistake," but the authors, both Goethe and Pieper, clearly mean something more generic here [translator's note].)

16. Simone Weil, *Gravity and Grace*, translated by Arthur Wills (New York: Farrar, Straus and Giroux, 1979), p. 121.

17. *ST* I/II 21, 4 ad 1.

18. *ST* I 63, 7 ad 2.

19. St. Anselm of Canterbury, *Cur Deus Homo* I, 15.

V: Pride and Desire

1. "Ratio culpae consistit in voluntaria aversione a Deo." *ST* II/II 34, 2; similarly, I 94, 1.

2. *ST* II/II 162, 6.

3. *ST* I/II 72, 2.

4. *ST* II/II 162, 6: "Aversio est formalis et completiva ratio pec-cati."

5. *De veritate* 3, 4 ad 5.

6. *ST* I/II 78, 1 ad 2; I 19, 9.

7. *De potentia* 3, 6 ad 14.

8. *ST* I/II 72, 2.

9. Aquinas, *Commentary on the Sentences* 2d. 42, 2, 1 ad 7.

10. Aquinas, *Quaestiones quodlibetiles* 5, 20.

11. *ST* II/II 20, 3.

12. *ST* I/II 84, 2.

13. Translator's note: At this point the author discusses the inadequacies of German for translating this important medieval Latin word. Because this issue might be somewhat distracting for the English-speaking reader I have placed the following sentence (with my comments in brackets) in this footnote: "*Begehrlichkeit* [literally, "greedy grasping," but with a rather old-fashioned connotation of "lustful longing"] is, I fear, a little too 'fresh' for it ever to claim a place in the living language."

14. *ST* I 63, 2.

15. *ST* III 8,7.

16. *ST* I/II 77, 4.

17. See in this context Aquinas's *Commentary on the Sentences* 2d, 42, 1, 5 ad 7.

18. C. S. Lewis, *The Problem of Pain* (New York: Macmillan, 1962).

19. Ibid., p. 81.

20. Ibid., p. 80.

VI: Mortal and Venial Sin

1. For example, *Gorgias* 515c.

2. See H. H. Janssen, *Schuld en Boeten in het oude Rome*.

3. *ST* I/II 88, 1: "Mortale et veniale opponuntur sicut reparabile et irreparabile."

4. *Nicomachean Ethics* 5, 8; 1136a.

5. *ST* I/II 88, 1 ad 1.

6. *ST* I/II 88, 6.

7. *ST* I/II 88, 1 ad 1.

8. *ST* I/II 77, 8 ad 1.

9. *ST* I/II 88, 1.

10. "The dictatorship of the proletariat entails the domination of the proletariat over the bourgeoisie, a domination that can-

not be limited by any law and is founded on force." Joseph Stalin, *Über die Grundlagen des Leninismus* (Berlin, 1946), p. 30 f.

11. Piet Schoonenberg, s.j., *Man and Sin: A Theological View*, translated by Joseph Donceel, s.j. (Notre Dame, Ind.: University of Notre Dame Press, 1965).

12. Ibid., p. 35.

13 Ibid., pp. 31, 37.

14. Aquinas, *Commentary on the Sentences* 2d. 42, 1, 5. The expression comes from the *Dialogues* of Gregory the Great.

15. Karl Rahner, *Schuld und Vergebung*, pp. 285 ff.

16. *Man and Sin*, p. 36.

17. Origen, *Commentary on the Book of Exodus*. Quoted in *Origen: Spirit and Fire, A Thematic Anthology of His Writings*, edited by Hans Urs von Balthasar, translated by Robert J. Daly, s.j. (Washington, D.C.: Catholic University of America Press), pp. 334–35.

VIII: The Paradox of Sin – A Freely Chosen Compulsion

1. J. M. Scheeben is even of the opinion that for this reason the name and concept of "deadly sin" has, strictly speaking, no content in the realm of natural ethics (Joseph Matthias Scheeben, *Die Mysterien des Christentums*, ed. Josef Höfer [Freiburg, 1941], p. 209).

2. Plato, *Meno* 99d.

3. *ST* I/II 58, 2; see also I/II 77, 2.

4. *Summa Contra Gentiles* 4, 92.

5. *De veritate* 15, 3 ad 2; ad 6.

6. *ST* I/II 79, 4.

7. *ST* 79, 3.

8. Ovid, *Metamorphoses* 7, 19: "Video meliora proboque deteriora sequor."

9. Virgil, *Georgics* I, 501.

10. Horace, *Odes* I, 3, 27.

11. Horace, *Epodes* 7, 18.

12. H. H. Janssen, *Schuld en Boeten en het oude Rome.*

13. Pascal, *Pensées* [Brunschwicg #434].

14. Immanuel Kant, *Religion within the Limits of Reason Alone*, translated by Theodore M. Greene and Hoyt H. Hudson (La Salle, Ill.: The Open Court Publishing Company, 1934), p. 38.

15. Ibid, p. 39.

16. Ibid., p. 73. (Kant is drawing on the memoirs of Pierre-François Xavier Charlevoix [1682–1761], a Jesuit missionary in Canada. [trans. note].)

17. Nicholai Hartmann, *Ethik*, p. 378.

18. *De veritate* 24, 3, ad 2.

19. *De veritate* 22, 6.

20. *De veritate* 24, 3 ad 2; *Commentary on the Sentences* 2d; 44, 1, 1 ad 1.

21. *De Veritate* 22,6.

22. *ST* I 62, 8 ad 3: ". . . peccare . . . pertinet ad defectum libertatis."

23. André Gide, *Tagebuch 1889–1939,* (Stuttgart, 1951), II: 257.

24. *ST* I/II 80, 9.

25. *ST* I 63, 1: "Quaecumque creatura rationalis, si in sua natura consideretur, potest peccare."

26. Ibid.

27. Ibid.

28. *De veritate* 18, 2 ad 5.

29. See Josef Pieper, "The Negative Element in the Philosophy of St. Thomas Aquinas," in: *The Silence of St. Thomas: Three Essays*, trans. by John Murray, s.j. and Daniel O'Connor (South Bend, Ind.: St. Augustine's Press, 1999), pp. 45–71.

30. *De veritate* 24, 8 ad 4.

31. *De veritate* 22, 6 ad 3; similarly *Commentary on the Sentences* 2d 23, 1.

VIII: The Stain of Sin

1. *ST* I/II 87, 6.

2. Plato, *Gorgias* 524e–525a.

3. *ST* I/II 86, 2 ad 1.

4. *ST* I/II 86 1 ad 1.

5. The reader might object that dirt does have a positive reality of its own. Perhaps the English term "sunspot" would help better convey the author's point in translation, for the word refers to what blocks the light on the sun's surface, not to anything ontologically different from the rest of the sun's chemistry (translator's note).

6. *ST* I/II 86, 2.

7. *ST* I/II 86, 2 ad 3: "Actus peccati facit distantiam a Deo."

8. *ST* II/II 37, 1; sed contra.

9. *De malo* 14, 2 ad 7.

10. André Gide, *Tagebuch* (1889–1939) 2: 187.

11. *De malo* 2, 11 ad 1; 2, 12.

12. See for example the *Oxford Latin Dictionary* of Lewis and Short (1958).

13. *De malo* 2, 3 ad 14.

14. Actually this holds true more for German than English, where the latter expression usually says "*worthy* of death" (translator's note).

15. Aquinas, *Commentary on the Sentences* 2d. 42, 1, 2.

16. Ibid., see also *De malo* 2, 2 ad 14.

17. Matthias Joseph Scheeben, *Mysterien des Christentums*, p. 239.

18. See, for example, Karl Prümm, *Der christliche Glaube und die altheidnische Welt* (Leipzig, 1935) 2: 243.

19. See Josef Pieper, *Death and Immortality*, translated by Richard and Clara Winston (South Bend, Ind.: St. Augustine's Press, 2000).

20. Plato, *Gorgias* 525c6.

21. Aquinas, *Commentary on the Sentences* 2d. 42, 1, 5.

22. *ST* I/II 87, 3 ad 1.

23. *ST* I/II 87, 4: "Amissio infiniti boni, scilicet Dei."

24. André Gide, *Tagebuch 1889–1939*, II: 187.

25. Fyodor Dostoyevsky, *The Brothers Karamazov*, Sixth Book, "A Russian Monk: From the Conversations and Sermons of the Hermit Sosima on Hell and Hellfire."

26. C. S. Lewis, *The Problem of Pain*, p. 118.

27. Ibid., p. 128.

28. *ST* I/II 80, 4 ad 3.

29. Nicholai Hartmann, *Ethik*, pp. 353 f.

30. Simone Weil, *Gravity and Grace*, p. 121.

31. *ST* III, 86, 1.

32. Friedrich Nietzsche, *The Gay Science* 3, 252.

33. Lao-tzu, *Tao-te-Ching* Part II, Chapter 71.

34. Plutarch, *Moralia*.

35. See Franz Seraph Steinleitner, *Die Beicht im Zusammenhange mit der sakralen Rechtspflege in der Antike* (Leipzig, 1913), pp. 75, 121.

36. Plato, *Gorgias* 480d.

37. Ibid., 481d.

Index